My Lakeland

A local lad's illustrated life
by Jim Watson

For Maureen, who's been with me all the way.

CONTENTS

8
PENRITH

18
POOLEY BRIDGE

24
ASKHAM

28
ULLSWATER
Aira Force, Glenridding,
Patterdale, Hartsop,
Brothers Water

42
THRELKELD
Blencathra

54
KESWICK
Keswick School, Sports,
Itchy feet, Castlerigg Stone Circle

70
RUGBY
Happy returns

74
DERWENT WATER
Grange, Rosthwaite, Seatoller,
Seathwaite, Newlands

94
COCKERMOUTH

100
BUTTERMERE VALLEY
Lorton, Loweswater,
Crummock Water, Buttermere

CONTENTS

110
BASSENTHWAITE & BACK O' SKIDDAW
Bassenthwaite, Uldale, Caldbeck, Hesket Newmarket

120
GRASMERE & THIRLMERE
Wordsworth, Rydal

130
AMBLESIDE & THE LANGDALES
Elterwater, Great Langdale, Little Langdale

146
WINDERMERE & BOWNESS
Troutbeck

162
HAWKSHEAD & CONISTON
Near Sawrey, Esthwaite Water, Tarn Hows, Coniston Water, Brantwood

178
RAVENGLASS & ESKDALE
La'al Ratty, Eskdale Green, Boot

186
WASDALE
Wasdale Head

192
THE PASSES
Kirkstone, Honister, Whinlatter, Dunmail Raise, Newlands Hause, Wrynose, Hardknott

Above: Typical Lakeland stone wall near Brothers Water.

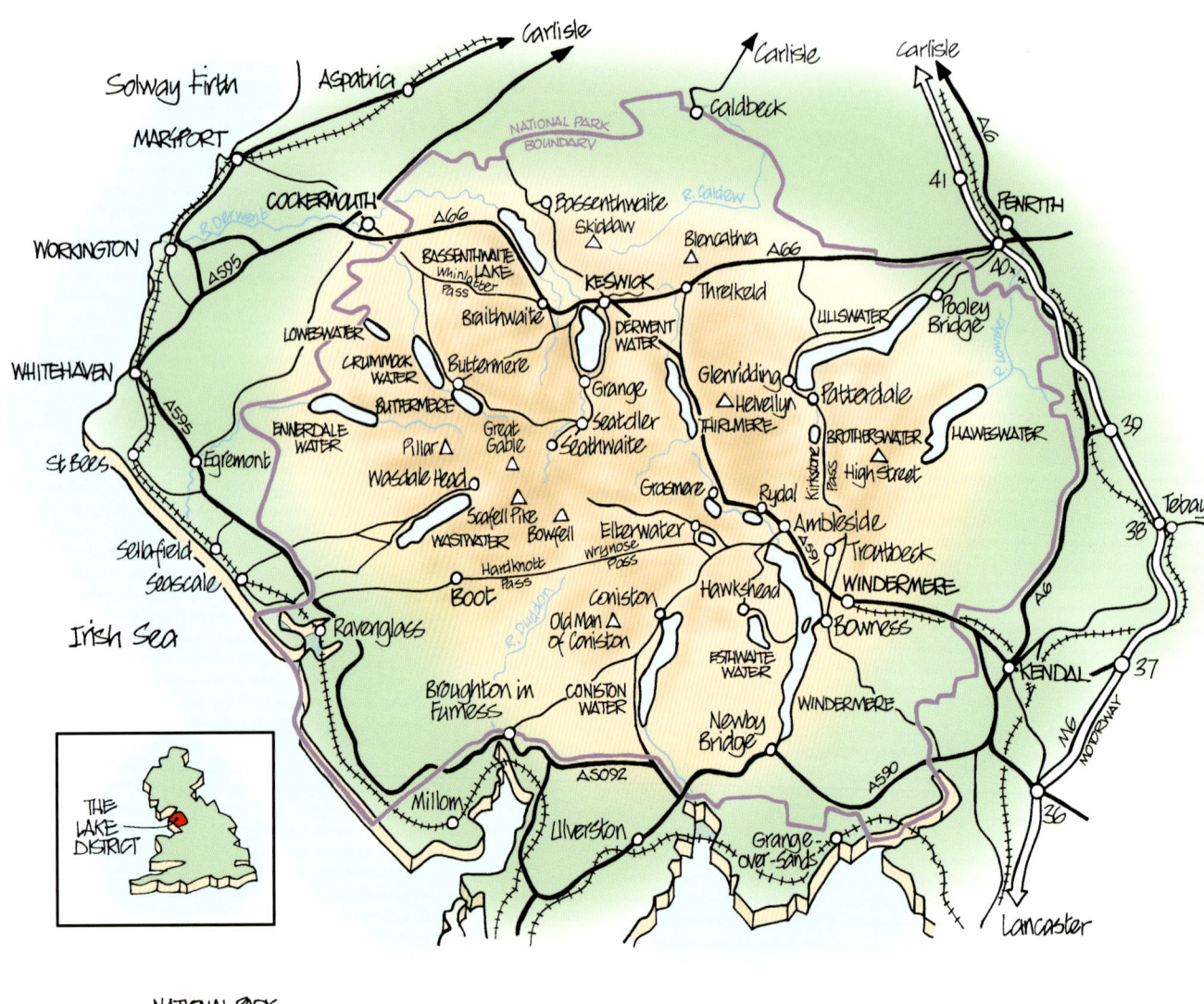

INTRODUCTION

> **❝** Lakeland is where dreams flourish uninhibited.

I've been friends with the Lake District for nigh-on 80 years. We've never fallen out – never had a bad word; though my friend's weather has on occasion pushed me to indiscretion.

At the age of 18 I deserted my friend for work and exile in the industrial midlands. The industry has long gone, but I'm still here.

While away, my relationship with the Lakes has deepened. Lakeland has become a dreamplace. A dreamplace I carry with me for comfort in an often uncomfortable world.

Though the largest of the English National Parks, the Lake District is only about 30 miles across and 40 miles from north to south – similar in size to Greater London. Traffic on the M6 speeds past in not much more than half-an-hour. Most drivers don't know what they're missing.

The mountains are high compared with others in England and the lakes are large in British terms, but on the world stage they're molehills and ponds. It's the variety and concentration of good things packed into such a small area that makes the Lake District so special; you don't have to travel far to be moved by something.

It was once said the Lake District was designed by angels. That's a bit over the top – even for a dreamer like me. Nevertheless, there's truth in it. Lakeland is where dreams flourish uninhibited.

This book is the culmination of those dreams; a compilation of the places I love. It's a personal collection inspired by a mix of childhood memories, nostalgia and the creation of hundreds of drawings. I've included historical bits and bobs that interest me as background information.

The many threats hanging over Lakeland have, over the years, been too often ignored. I don't want threats to my dreams: no traffic, crowds, litter, poverty, second homes, unemployment, off-road 4x4s or a multitude of big-footed developers eager to stamp on this landscape of delights. I'll leave the fights to other folk: those with bigger voices.

Compiling this book has been a labour of love and confirmed to me that Lakeland is definitely my Hotel California.

I've checked out but I can never leave.

Jim Watkins

Rugby, 2022.

Penrith

Birth, toffee and Grandma's gossip

The bustling market town of Penrith is unlike the rest of Lakeland. It's not in the National Park and it's built of red sandstone. Set in the rolling hills of the Eden valley stretching north from the River Eamont to Carlisle, the town has been a crossroads for centuries.

The A6 – once the main highway between London and Scotland – and the A66 trans-Pennine link between West Cumbria and the A1 cross here. Penrith also has a mainline railway station, now with 'North Lakes' added to its name to attract the tourist trade.

The M6 motorway runs close to the town reducing urban traffic, but Penrith still boasts an 'interesting' one way system around the streets.

Dominating central Penrith is the Musgrave Monument, erected by public subscription in 1861 as a memorial to Philip Musgrave, eldest son of the town's benefactor family who died tragically, aged 26, in Spain. Despite architectural critic Nikolaus Pevsner dismissing it as 'insignificant', local people still affectionately refer to it as 'T' Clock'.

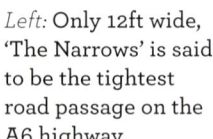

Left: Only 12ft wide, 'The Narrows' is said to be the tightest road passage on the A6 highway.

HSBC · 'The Narrows' · Arnisons, the drapers, established in 1740. It was once the home of William Wordsworth's grandparents

On his way south to claim the English throne in 1745, Bonny Prince Charlie is said to have stayed at the George Hotel, the solemn sandstone building stretching across the east side of Devonshire Street.

Three impressive bank buildings cluster around T' Clock, competing for attention with wildly differing architectural styles. Barclays goes way over the top with sandstone Gothic, while NatWest is cool in white marble. Most handsome is the classically styled HSBC.

Above: Devonshire Street, T' Clock and the HSBC.
Right: Barclays Bank.

PENRITH

Above: **Little Dockray.**

Penrith has a long and often violent history. Once part of Scotland, it was seized for England by Edward I in 1295. Fifteen years of border skirmishes followed, with Penrith burnt to the ground on three occasions. The Scottish marauders were finally brought to heel by a garrison of troops stationed in the rebuilt castle.

The town's layout – a confusion of small squares, or 'gates', connected by narrow streets, passages and alleys – was developed as a defence against border raids.

Little Dockray is an interesting byway off Devonshire Street with a pub, gallery, bookshop, various coffee shops and cafés, plus plenty of quirky buildings for me to draw. A cycle and toy shop on the corner has been there since… well… since I was a lad. Characterless shops now line Middlegate, which was once inhabited by 17th-century weavers, tanners and tailors.

PENRITH

The lintel on Robinson's School displays the date 1670, though the building may be older. Its founder, Penrith-born William Robinson, died in 1660 after making his fortune in London. He left £55 a year to the town, £20 of which would be spent specifically on the 'education and upbringing of girls'.

They were housed on the upper floor and were taught the three Rs plus spinning and weaving. Boys were kept out until 1770. The poorest scholars wore badges lettered 'PS' that allowed them to beg in the streets. They had a miserable time, enduring 11-hour working days and frequent beatings. A new 'rod of chastisement' was supplied to the school each week.

Schooling of a less brutal nature carried on here until 1970. Since 1990 the building has housed the town's local history museum. A Tourist Information Centre was tagged on in 1989.

Grandma used to take me shopping in Penrith, where she'd catch up with local gossip. Wide-eared, I'd stand close, eagerly absorbing a catalogue of scandal and saucy goings-on. For a treat we'd go to the cinema, buying toffee to scoff during the performance. Remarkably the toffee shop (like the cinema) is still there!

Whenever I'm in town I like to buy something to remember those carefree days with Grandma. Sadly, I'm now a denture wearer (the result of too many sweets, I suppose), so sucking toffee is a major undertaking. That said, I usually rise to the occasion.

Above: **The Toffee Shop in Brunswick Road.**
Below: **The Tourist Information Centre on the far left, Robinson School in the middle and the Alhambra Cinema in Middlegate.**

PENRITH

The sandstone Church of St Andrew dates from 1720. It's grand and square – like a huge slab of rich brown fruitcake. Three galleries inside are supported on Tuscan columns, while two brass chandeliers were given to the town by the Duke of Portland for its support in the 1745 Jacobite rebellion.

The first time I set foot in the impressive church interior was for Granda's funeral in 1979. It was no more than he deserved.

The Giant's Grave in the churchyard always fascinated me as we walked along the lane by the church on our way to the buses in Sandgate. It consists of two 11th-century stone crosses connected by four hogback tombstones.

The length of the grave suggests its occupant was almost 12ft tall. Archaeologists say that's absurd, and it's actually a mass grave. Who cares? I still believe there's a giant down there.

Bishop Yards curves attractively around the south side of the churchyard past an elegant Georgian town house – a surprise amongst all the sandstone. Next to it stands the imposing Church Rooms, built on the site of a cock-fighting pit where raucous crowds reputedly drowned out the vicar's sermons in the church.

Above: Bishop Yards.
Below: Giant's Grave.

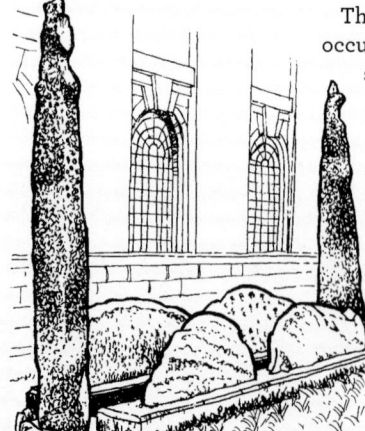

PENRITH

◀ Near the church, Sandgate once rang with the sounds of bear-baiting. Penrith was known for its ferocious bull terriers. Baying crowds were kept well lubricated at numerous inns around the square.

I remember Sandgate as the town's bus terminus, where people climbed aboard red double-deckers heading for exotic-sounding places like Shap and Lazonby. Meanwhile, great white stratocruiser coaches roared away to far-flung foreign parts – Newcastle and Manchester.

▶ Sandgate is linked to Middlegate by Burrowgate, where most of one side of the street was once Co-operative shops.

Mysterious hissing pipes rose from the counters. Grandma's payment was put into a canister and sucked up into a metal network that ran across the ceiling. After a wait – during which the weather was discussed, various illnesses diagnosed and surprise shown over how much I'd grown since last week – the canister would clatter back through the pipes into a wire basket. Inside was Grandma's change. What a palaver – but endlessly fascinating to a small boy.

◀ The town's oldest and most interesting buildings cluster around the church (*far left*), with many dating from the 1700s. A preserved Tudor building (*right*) is part of Anne Birkett's Dame School that William Wordsworth, then aged five, attended while staying with his grandparents. There he first met local tobacconist's daughter Mary Hutchinson, who became his wife 27 years later.

His mother, Ann, daughter of a Penrith linen draper, died aged 30 after a visit to London in 1778. A year later eight-year-old William was sent to school in Hawkshead.

Wordsworth's relationship with Penrith was not yet over. Fifteen years later, while nursing a consumptive friend, Raisley Calvert, at Keswick, it was decided Calvert needed a warmer climate. The two men set off for Lisbon, but only reached Penrith, where Raisley died at the Robin Hood Inn.

PENRITH

Predictably, corn used to be sold in the Cornmarket, west of T' Clock. The Market Cross was built in 1983. Though simply a Westmorland slated roof supported on wooden pillars, it is both effective and beautiful, popular with market traders, the town band and love-struck teenagers.

The nearby Board & Elbow inn guards the corner into Great Dockray like an impenetrable fortress. The broad square was the town's beast market in the 18th century. Now a car park, it still hosts a weekly market – though now without the livestock.

Below: **The Market Cross and Board & Elbow inn in Great Dockray.**

▶ Currently an inn and restaurant, Dockray Hall in Great Dockray was for 150 years The Gloucester Arms in tribute to Richard Neville, Duke of Gloucester. He stayed here around 1471 while the castle was being made habitable for him.

In 1483, at the age of 31, Neville was crowned King Richard the Third, only to be killed two years later at the Battle of Bosworth Field.

Dockray Hall was built by Neville's grandfather and is rumoured to have had a 300-yard-long tunnel to the castle.

PENRITH

Now a major historic relic, Penrith Castle was originally a 14th-century pele tower, built as a bastion against Scottish raids.

In 1471 it was added to by Richard Neville, who lived in the large, draughty castle before becoming king. It fell out of use during the 16th century and the sandstone blocks were plundered for building material.

Ullswater Road has taken some of the deep castle moat, but most of it remains, and is much enjoyed by small children who like to roll down its sides. Flymo mowers must have been godsends for the park gardeners.

Beyond the ruins there are tennis courts and a bowling green set amongst attractive gardens.

Top: The 'Black Angel' Boar War memorial in the park.
Above: The castle from Ullswater Road.

◀ Penrith station lies across the road from the castle. Built of sandstone and slate in the mid-19th century, it's looking a bit dated now, but still boasts long, curving platforms.

During construction of the railway between Lancaster and Carlisle, there was for many years a break in the line while engineers figured out how best to cross the Shap fells. Eventually – and with the considerable help of 10,000 English, Scots and Irish workers – the bleak obstacle was crossed and the main line completed in 1846.

PENRITH

On three sides Penrith is hilly. The A6 climbs north out of the town towards Carlisle, while terraces of sandstone houses rise steeply in the east to Beacon Edge.

Castlegate, the steepest part of the town's interminable one-way system, sweeps upwards from the Cornmarket passing bars, bistros and ancient terraced housing to the castle and – equally substantial in ubiquitous sandstone – the Station Hotel.

There used to be a terrific steam museum at the top of Castlegate and I spent many happy hours drawing the magnificent traction engines for my *Lakeland Towns* book. Sadly, it's long gone.

Also closed is the nearby agricultural market. Granda knew a lot of farmers and he used to take me with him when he dropped in for t' crack. One of the old buildings is now occupied by the Penrith Players Theatre, established in 1922, an amateur group run by volunteers.

Penrith's famous Beacon is prominently set overlooking the town on the 937ft-high summit of a series of sand dunes that straggle

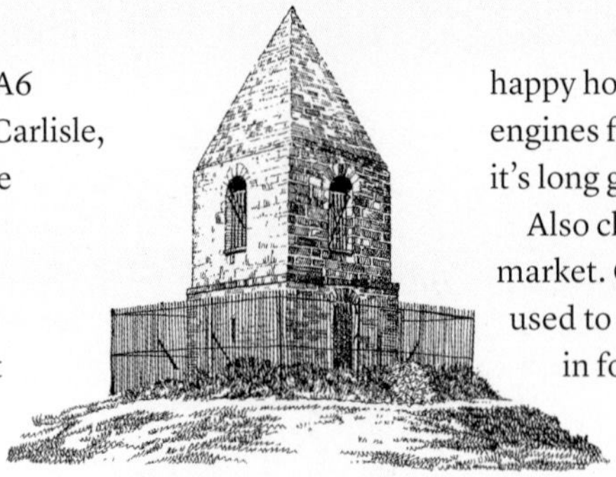

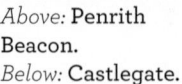

Above: **Penrith Beacon.**
Below: **Castlegate.**

NEWBIGGIN

eastwards to the Pennines. A beacon was recorded here in 1468 – once a link in an invasion early-warning system across the country.

The present Beacon dates from 1719, restored in 1780 as a monument to the town's involvement in the 1745 Jacobite rebellion. It's as tall as a modern semi and, despite high railings, the sandstone is pitted with names and dates scratched by determined visitors.

Impressive though it is, the Beacon cannot match the extensive view across the town to the Ullswater fells and Blencathra. Penrith always seems quite distant from Lakeland in character, but, as this view demonstrates, geographically it's close.

Like much else, the town has changed a lot during my lifetime, though its friendly disposition seems undiminished.

Penrith is no better for being my birthplace, but I like to think that by starting here my life has been enriched.

Newbiggin

On retirement my grandparents moved to a council house at Newbiggin, a small village three miles west of Penrith. I loved to spend time there, relishing the luxury of a house with three bedrooms, a kitchen and a bathroom. Granda insisted on a daily walk and I was happy to join him, often climbing to the top of Flusco Pike, a limestone outcrop only around 150ft above the village, but with great views.

Newbiggin was transformed in the early 19th century when large-scale quarrying of limestone began. The stone was initially used for railway ballast and in the construction industry, but when found to have greater financial value as a constituent of mortar and as a fertiliser, huge kilns were constructed to calcine the stone into lime at Flusco quarry and Blencow, on the edge of the village.

The Penrith to Cockermouth railway was opened in 1865 with a station at Newbiggin and sidings for the Blencow and Flusco limeworks. The line sloped down to Penrith and there were numerous tales of 'escaping' wagons from Blencow mysteriously appearing in Penrith station. No injuries were recorded.

Newbiggin enjoyed a boom time, with workers even travelling on the railway to work in the quarry at Threlkeld.

The quarries and limeworks were an ugly blot on the landscape and the human cost must also have been considerable. My grandparents' neighbour worked at Blencow and used to cycle home engulfed in a cloud of lime dust. I hope Bob lived to a ripe old age, but doubt it. The limeworks closed in the 1960s and the railway was dismantled in 1970.

▲ I was born at 30 Brunswick Square, Penrith, then an ordinary terrace house that served as a private nursing home in those wartime, pre-NHS days. It cost 12 guineas for a fortnight's confinement – quite a sum in 1942. Quite a confinement too, compared with today's lightening turnarounds. My father was told of my arrival while riding in a professional cycle race at Bampton Sports, 15 miles away.

Top left: **Flusco limeworks.**
Top centre: **Blencow limeworks.**

Pooley Bridge

Finkle Street, bullheads and lake trips

Pooley Bridge is situated at the north end of Ullswater, where the River Eamont flows out of the lake to eventually join the River Eden at Langwathby. The village has been a crossing place for centuries, originally via stepping stones from which nets were cast into a large pool to catch fish. This gave Pooley a vital industry and its name. 'Bridge' was added in 1800.

A market for fish, cattle and sheep was established in the square and at one time Pooley was more important than Penrith.

The elegant three-arched stone bridge was built in 1764, with the river later becoming part of the boundary between the old counties of Cumberland and Westmorland. During unprecedented flooding following Storm Desmond in December 2015, the bridge collapsed.

A temporary footbridge was erected in March 2016 and replaced in May 2020 by the UK's first stainless steel road bridge. It was opened for vehicular traffic on 23 October, 2020, when a ceremonial flock of 150 sheep became the first to cross it.

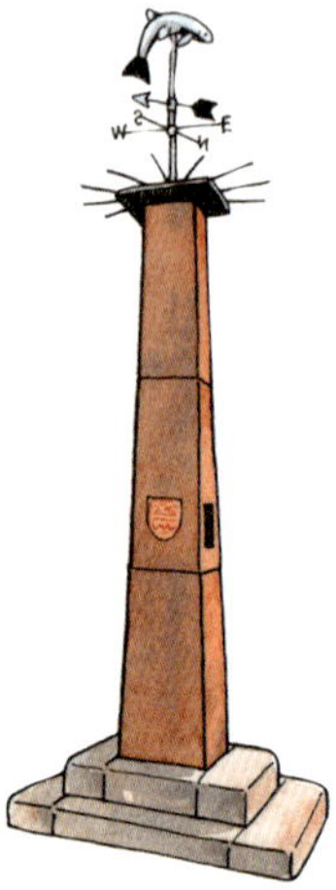

After my Penrith birth, my mother brought me back to the family home in Pooley Bridge. We lived in an 18th-century end-of-terrace cottage in Finkle Street, a narrow cul-de-sac off the square. Don't rush there to see the blue plaque; the cottage was demolished soon after we left as being unfit for human habitation. A double garage was built in its place.

Our only downstairs room was sparsely equipped, with an open fire, a small Baby Belling cooker, an electric kettle and a sink. Food was stored in a larder under the stairs where the mice often got to it before we did. Two bedrooms up a winding staircase completed our family home.

There was no bathroom, no garden and the toilet was at the end of a narrow alley outside with a mangle for company and damp editions of the *Daily Mirror* for toilet paper. I have no idea how my mother washed our clothes, though I do recollect her hanging them out to dry in the street.

Above: **The Millennium Cross erected on the square to celebrate Pooley's fishing village origins.**
Below: **Pooley Bridge in 2020.**

POOLEY BRIDGE

I was a sickly, asthmatic child who spent too much time in bed, fortified by comics and tablets that did little for my asthma but made me sleep a lot. A doctor decided removing my tonsils would help, so I had them taken out in Carlisle hospital. The medically approved recuperation was to stay in bed and eat lots of ice cream. I had no problem following those orders, as my love of ice cream holds no bounds and I had the additional pick-me-up of the newly published *Eagle* comic to drool over. The artwork – some in colour and mainly by Frank Hampson – was (and still is) stunning. I remember thinking: "I'd like to do that." The journey had begun.

One of my earliest recollections is of the hard winter of 1947, when I was just five. After heavy snowfall my father opened the front door one morning and all you could see was snow, which had drifted down the street and piled as high as our upstairs windows. Somehow he managed to dig us out – a superhuman achievement as the only digging implement in the house was a shovel used to put coal on the fire.

Above: **Pooley Bridge 1764–2015.**
Below: **Finkle Street.**

19

POOLEY BRIDGE

Above: **A rare quiet day at Pooley Bridge.**

After two baby brothers joined the family, our house became seriously overcrowded, so I spent a lot of time outside or visiting other, more spacious households.

In one of them, two old ladies used to hide a sweet for me to find amongst their huge collection of ceramic ornaments.

Meanwhile, the house next door – now the village shop – was occupied by country sports enthusiasts. Here I had to stand on a leather couch amongst preserved heads of foxes and tail brushes to sing a chorus of 'D'ye Ken John Peel?' before being given a sweet.

A single sweet might seem modest reward, but in those days confectionary was still subject to wartime rationing and was therefore a valuable commodity, especially to a sweet-tooth like me. Sweet rationing finally ended in February 1953.

My grandfather was the village policeman. His family – Grandma, three sons and my mother – lived in the cramped police house on the square. The front room was dedicated to police business, with a living room and scullery to the rear. A back garden stretched to the river, where Granda spent much of his off-duty time growing vegetables to feed the family.

I recall the novelty of a telephone being installed in Granda's office. Set on a lace doily at the centre of a highly polished table, it was a scary, alien object to me – and I suspect for Granda as well. With much finger-wagging I was given strict instructions what to do if it began to ring.

After that I only entered the room with extreme caution and always rushed past the phone, fearing it would suddenly burst into life. I've disliked answering phones ever since.

> **If that rings – don't touch it!**

Granny Dowbekin's Tearoom

Hunters Cottage. The former police house

POOLEY BRIDGE

Above: **Pooley Bridge Inn.**
Below: **The western side of the square.**

In the 1950s Pooley Bridge was a sedate place, populated almost entirely by elderly people. The only child in the village of my age was Nancy, the youngest daughter of the family who owned the Chalet Hotel, a distinctive building on the edge of the square.

These days the Chalet is the Pooley Bridge Inn, with a perennially busy beer garden. Back then, old gents sat on the lawn reading newspapers and calling for quiet as Nancy and I raced around the veranda and thumped the keys of the piano in the dining room.

My number one playmate was the bridge; a bit odd you might think, but some of my happiest times occurred either on, under or around its ancient buttresses.

Using rocks and pieces of turf I liked to dam a beck that joined the river at the bridge. The challenge was to see how long my dam would hold back the water before being swept away. I never dreamt that a similar fate on a grand scale would befall the bridge itself some 70 years later.

I loved to paddle in the fresh water with soft waterweed and fish swirling around my feet. Otters scrambling into the western bank were a familiar sight.

Catching minnows was a regular pastime. A wine bottle 'procured' from the Crown Hotel yard made a useful minnow trap with a hole knocked in the dimple, or 'punt', in the bottom and pieces of bread as bait. A particularly treasured catch was a bullhead which, unlike the sleek and shiny minnows, is a rough and ugly fish that lives under rocks.

Village stores

POOLEY BRIDGE

There were rowing boat landings near the steamer pier where I spent many a summer's day admiring well-to-do tourists rowing out onto the lake. When older, though still only about nine, I was allowed to park the boats after the visitors had come ashore.

The landing stages were dismantled years ago and in 1965 a pumping station for taking water from the lake to Haweswater was built. It's now a pleasant viewpoint with seats and a beautifully carved memorial to Lord Birkett QC who, in 1962, was instrumental in saving the lake from being turned it into a reservoir and the water level being raised by nearly three feet. An inscription on the memorial, '*Si Monumentum Requiris Circumspice*', is taken from Christopher Wren's monument in St Paul's Cathedral. It translates as: "If you seek his memorial – look around you."

And that's exactly what I enjoyed doing at the boat landings and from the steamer pier. The view down the broad part of the lake to Howtown and the distant mountains was, and still is, one of my favourites, promising so much for anyone who ventures south into this blessed corner of the Lake District.

Pooley Bridge has always catered for its visitors, and in recent years has applied itself to the task with gusto. Old houses have been done up as holiday lets, pubs have been modernised and extended, lavish beer gardens have sprung up around the square and along the riverside, car parks have been created and the new multi-million pound bridge opened. Eating, drinking and souvenir trinkets abound. There's even a gin distillery. The only things missing are peace and quiet.

Maybe I'm the grump in the corner, but I cherish my memories and, looking back, my early childhood in the village was something special. Despite all that's happened to the place since, I'll keep visiting. Pooley will always hold a special place in my heart.

▲ Captain Band lived in Finkle Street and on occasion would take me for a trip up and down the lake on his steamer – as romantic and exciting to a small boy as crossing the Atlantic. From the pier at Pooley (*above*), the drama gradually built as we travelled through the lake's three reaches to the final climactic stretch, cruising into Glenridding, surrounded by high fells, as if it was New York.

> **Pooley will always hold a special place in my heart.**

Below: **View south from the pier.**

Yanwath School

I started at the local primary school, Yanwath, when I was five. It wasn't all that local – it was three miles away – but we had a school bus service. I thought the bus very grand, comfortable, and you didn't have to pay. Yanwath school is still there and still teaching primary children. Though it's been extended and modernised, I can still pick out parts of the old building.

My teacher throughout my time there was Miss Brown, a Scottish spinster.

Grey hair collected in a tight bun, long skirts, a no-nonsense blouse and an ever-present woollen cardigan suggested a forbidding disposition, but she did have a kindly side – usually kept well-hidden.

When my mother questioned her about my terrible spelling her stock answer was, "It's not the brain – it's the character that counts," something I still trot out whenever my spelling is questioned.

I was chuffed when a Miss Brown lookalike began to appear in the Bash Street Kids comic strip in *The Beano*. Years later I did illustration work for the publishers, DC Thomson, but sadly never got to draw my Miss Brown.

Yanwath had a strictly no-nonsense approach to education and discipline. I'm left-handed so suffered regular raps across the knuckles with a ruler, accompanied with a stern "Use the other hand, laddie!" from Miss Brown.

It didn't work.

> **We all stood as a sniffling boy was brought forward.**

The ultimate school discipline was exercised one morning when the whole school, including teachers, was assembled. We all stood as a sniffling boy was brought forward. The headmaster produced a leather strap cut into tails at the end and energetically whacked three sharp lashes to both of the boy's hands.

I have no recollection of what he'd done to deserve such treatment; the horror of his public chastisement seems to have erased it from my memory. Almost unbelievably now, a leather strap was the standard implement of punishment in state schools until 1987.

Occasionally, a travelling picture show called at the school. It was a converted furniture van with a large screen in the back onto which silent films were projected. We all trooped outside with our chairs, come rain or shine. Neither was the ideal condition – it was either too wet or too bright – but being able to watch the grainy antics of Laurel and Hardy or Charlie Chaplin was immeasurably preferable to watching a boy being strapped.

Another horror (at least for me) was having to walk hand in hand (*with a girl!*) to the nearby village of Tirril where we had to participate in (*gasp!*) country dancing!

'Nuff said.

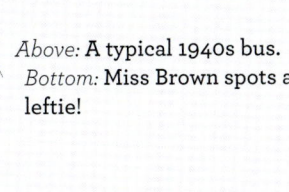

Above: **A typical 1940s bus.**
Bottom: **Miss Brown spots a leftie!**

Askham

Picturesque personified and a spendthrift Lowther

Three miles east of Pooley Bridge, but far away in character, lies the tranquil village of Askham. Whenever I tire of Lakeland honeypots this is one of my refuges.

The village's mile-long main street runs west to east downhill from the limestone slopes of Askham Fell to the River Lowther, crossed at the mid-point by the Penrith to Haweswater road.

Delightful vernacular cottages and farmhouses, many dating to the 17th century, line Askham's spacious greens. Some are set on grassy banks, displayed like trophies in a collection of desirable country residences. Magnificent trees overhang the verges and frame wonderful compositions.

Above: **Clark Hill doorway.**
Below: **A superb vernacular panorama.**

Askham was bought by the powerful Lowther family in 1724 as part of their extensive development of Cumberland. Their influence has maintained it as a working village without destroying its old-world charm. Many residents work for Lowther Estates.

Lowther Park has been a working farm since 1283 with a long history of local, sustainable food production. Three thousand acres are farmed organically, and meat, fish, game and vegetables from the Lowther rivers, woods and moors are menu mainstays at the estate's inns, the George and Dragon at Clifton, three miles away, and The Queen's Head in Askham.

Once a 14th-century defensive tower, imposing Askham Hall overlooks the River Lowther. It was converted to a mansion in Elizabethan times by Thomas Sandford, whose family lived there until it became a rectory.

For many years it was home to the Lowther family, who moved there when the castle was abandoned in 1957. It's now a luxury hotel with gardens and café open to the public. The present eighth Earl lives at Thrimby, a few miles south of Lowther Park.

There are 57 listed buildings in Askham including the 1897 limestone ashlar bridge over the Lowther, the stone gateposts to Askham Hall, three lime kilns and a 1935 red phone box.

Askham also has a friendly corner shop and two cosy pubs, The Punchbowl and The Queen's Head, where the clientele seem content to chat rather than party. On the Penrith road there's a public hall and (*brrr*) an open-air swimming pool.

Above: **The lower green and distant Lowther Castle.**
Below: **Askham Hall.**

ASKHAM

Askham is not your typical Lakeland village. There's none of the green slate walls of Elterwater or Rosthwaite here. Set on the eastern edge of the National Park, Askham doesn't feel much like Lakeland either – even though Ullswater's only a few miles away.

The architectural historian and critic Nikolaus Pevsner describes Askham as "of the North Riding type", and you can see what he means.

Above: **Park View Cottage.**
Bottom: **The White Cottage.**

However, this village is unique. The houses are of widely differing designs, shapes and sizes, some even on different levels, but they all fit together perfectly – each contributing to a hugely satisfying overall picture. And there's room for the wonderful trees to flourish, too.

I never have a problem finding something to draw at Askham. It's what to leave out that's difficult.

 I never have a problem finding something to draw at Askham. It's what to leave out that's difficult.

ASKHAM

One of the largest landowners in the Lake District, the Lowther family are known throughout Cumbria. James, the first Earl of Lonsdale, brought the industrial revolution to his West Cumberland coalfields, building most of Whitehaven.

Lowther Castle, the ostentatious seat of the Lowther family, was completed in 1814. It's a fine example of Gothic Revival architecture, the first work by Robert Smirke who went on to design the British Museum. Some 420ft wide and with a variety of turrets and towers reminiscent of a fairytale castle, even in ruin it's a remarkable sight.

Set on a ridge overlooking the River Lowther are two more memorials to the family in their 19th-century pomp. St Michael's Church, dating from 1686, is the family chapel, packed with memorials to sundry Lowthers. The Gothic, Hammer Films-style mausoleum of William the second Earl, who died in 1844, is nearby. Inside there's a marble effigy of him sitting in gloomy isolation behind a panel of thick glass.

Above: **Lord Lonsdale – the 'Yellow Earl' – 1857–1944.**

◀ From 1880 to 1944 lord of the manor was the fifth Earl, Hugh – last of the Lowther big spenders. A sporting legend, he left the famous Lonsdale belts for boxing as one of his bequests. The colour yellow was another passion. Cars, servants, and the Automobile Association – of which he was first president – were all decked in yellow. On his death, Hugh left huge debts and the castle in disrepair. The decline was irreversible and in 1958 much of the castle was demolished, leaving only the façade we see today. Subsequent Earls have restored the fortunes of Lowther Park, which, with its romantic ruins, gardens and piazza-style café, is now one of Lakeland's most popular attractions.

Top right: **The Mausoleum and St Michael's Church.**
Below: **Lowther Castle.**

Ullswater

Bluebird, daffodils and William's legs

Ullswater is the shape of an elongated 'Z', with three distinct reaches. There's the gentle landscape at the northern Pooley Bridge end, a more scenic central section and then the full-on grandeur and mountain magnificence of the southern reach around Glenridding.

Ullswater snakes its way through the landscape for around seven and a half miles. It's almost a mile wide and 205ft deep, with five small islands, all at the southern end. The steamers call at four piers around the lake.

Place Fell
2,154ft (657m)

Hartsop Dodd
2,018ft (615m)

Arnison Crag
1,424ft (434m)

Stoney Cove Pike
2502ft (763m)

Birks
2,040ft (622m)

Silver Crag

Ullswater

ULLSWATER

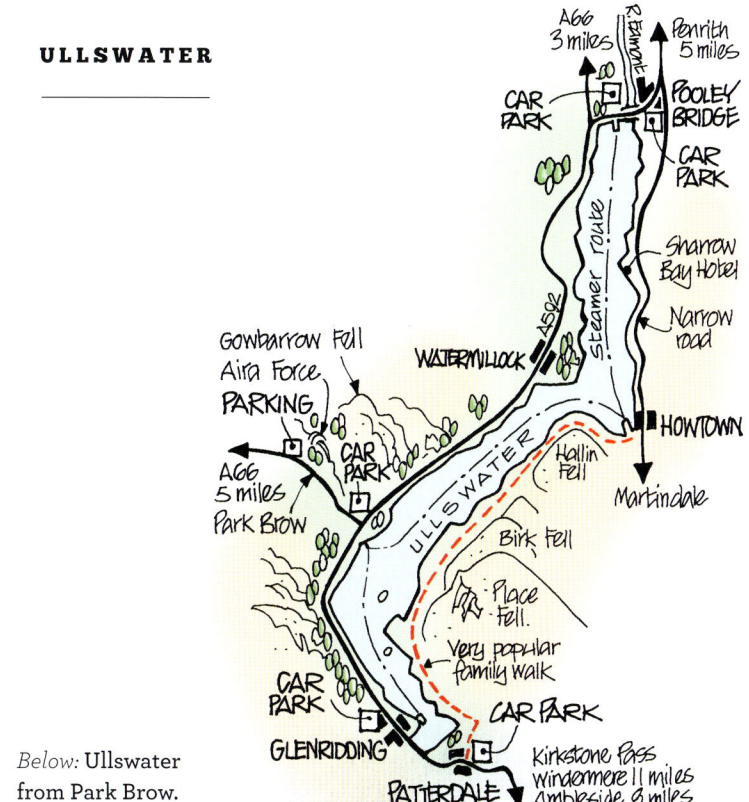

An ongoing Lakeland controversy is which is the 'better' lake, Ullswater or Derwent Water. From Pooley Bridge to Howtown, Ullswater is all about the lake. Then the mountains begin to feature and that lovely bend around Place Fell promises a dramatic climax. The southern reach is all about the mountains. The spectacle is so overpowering, the lake doesn't get much of a look in.

Derwent Water, on the other hand, is *all* about the lake – the twists and turns of the shoreline, the islands and the woods; here the mountains are bit players. You can also walk around practically all of the shoreline, which has always nudged it into prime position in the 'better lake' debate to me.

Below: Ullswater from Park Brow.

ULLSWATER

In 1955 Donald Campbell set the world water speed record when he piloted his jet-propelled hydroplane Bluebird K7 to a speed of 202.32mph across Ullswater.

Earlier in his campaign we decided to witness this phenomenon, so astride our rubbish-tip bikes we fearlessly rode the 11 miles from Threlkeld to Ullswater like Hells Angels on Harleys. We didn't know for sure if Bluebird would be having an outing, but a few miles from the lake we could hear it was – the noise from the jet engine was unbelievable. The volume built until we reached Park Brow, where the thundering sound wailed and echoed around the fells.

> **We rode the 11 miles from Threlkeld to Ullswater like Hells Angels on Harleys.**

When our ears became used to the racket, we became instant jet boat experts, discussing the merits of choosing the lake's shortest reach to travel at 200mph. As we lounged on the grass at Park Brow, we also wondered how good Bluebird's brakes were. Would they stop the boat's headlong streak, or would it end halfway up Gowbarrow Fell?

Thankfully we all survived the day and made it home without major breakdowns.

When my mother asked me what I'd been doing all day I gave her my stock answer: "Nowt, really." If she'd known I'd been witnessing history in the making, she'd only have worried…

Arthur's Pike
1,747ft (532m)

Loadpot Hill

Bonscale Pike
1,718ft (524m)

Wether Hill
2,210ft (674m)

High Street
2,718ft (828m)

Swarthbeck Gill

Ullswater

Howtown

ULLSWATER

When I lived at Pooley Bridge, the wooded hill overlooking the village was called Dunmallet by all and sundry. Even Wainwright called it that in his *Outlying Fells of Lakeland* in 1974. Since then the name has mysteriously morphed into Dunmallard.

A similar transformation took place with 'Derwentwater'. For years it was a single word; now it's two – 'Derwent Water'. Which begs the question why isn't Ullswater 'Ulls Water'?

There are other examples of this restyling of names throughout the Lakes, but who decides that a change is necessary – and why are such changes so readily adopted?

Right: Martindale Hause hairpins.
Below: Ullswater from the Brackenrigg Inn.

Steel Knotts 1,414ft (431m)
The Nab 1,887ft (575m)
Watermillock
Martindale
Beda Fell 1,664ft (507m)
Hallin Fell 1,271ft (387m)
Angletarn Pikes 1,857ft (566m)
Place Fell 2,154ft (656m)
St Sunday Crag 2,756ft (840m)
The Knotts

Hallin Fell
Dunmallet
Ullswater
Howtown
Arthur's Pike
Bonscale Pike

Aira Force

A half-mile before entering Ullswater, gentle Aira Beck turns into a wild waterfall, Aira Force, plunging 65ft into a picturesque fairy dell much loved by Victorian tourists and many more since. A small arched bridge spans the stream above the waterfall and provides a spectacular viewpoint as the water gathers for its leap. A second bridge at the bottom allows you to get close to the action.

Since I was a child Aira Force has impressed me, and the woodland setting is fabulous.

The lake shoreline below Aira Force is where in 1802 William Wordsworth and his sister Dorothy saw the wild daffodils that inspired the poet's most famous poem. A gate near the National Trust tearoom celebrates Dorothy's writing and her considerable influence on the poetry of her brother.

'Daffodils' was penned after Dorothy and William visited Eusemere, a country house at Pooley Bridge – home of the anti-slavery campaigner Thomas Clarkson. They were returning to Grasmere, a journey of 15 miles as the crow flies – which could have included a 2,000ft climb on the old packhorse road over Grisedale Hause. They would have been carrying luggage and wearing ordinary clothes, rather than hundreds of pounds worth of gear from an Ambleside outdoor shop.

The popular caricature of the wimpy Romantic poets is blown away by their prodigious walks. Robert Southey is said to have regularly visited the Wordsworths – walking from Keswick to Grasmere and taking in Helvellyn on the way.

William and Dorothy were phenomenal walkers. De Quincey, in his *Recollections of the Lake Poets*, calculated that Wordsworth's legs "must have traversed a distance of 175 to 180,000 English miles".

GLENRIDDING

Slopes of Birkhouse Moor

Sheffield Pike 2,232ft (680m)

Stybarrow Dodd 2,770ft (844m)

Slopes of Glenridding Dodd

Above: Glenridding from the lakeside.

Glenridding

Previously one of the UK's most prosperous mining villages, Glenridding is now a walker's mecca, starting point for a number of famous routes, particularly along Striding Edge onto Helvellyn. The village was difficult to reach until 1926, when part of Stybarrow Crag was blasted away to make the lakeside road. ...And so the flood of visitors began.

The village is little more than a couple of rows of former miners' cottages set back from the lake, a store, numerous tearooms and B&Bs plus a couple of up-market hotels.

Gold and silver were found here in the 19th century, but the Greenside mine at the head of Glenridding Beck was exceptionally rich in lead. The mines were worked out by 1962 after a record 300 years of continuous production.

▼ The Travellers Rest inn stands high above Glenridding with a splendid view over the village and Ullswater. How welcoming it must have been for miners after hours underground – though I doubt thirsty miners spent much time admiring the view.

33

STEAMERS

The steamers

The steamers are a popular Ullswater attraction, providing regular trips up and down the lake and calling at Pooley Bridge, Howtown, Aira Force and Glenridding 363 days a year. In the 1850s the steamers were working boats, moving mail, workers and goods to and from the Greenside lead mine. Today there are five heritage vessels – now diesel powered – plying the tourist trade.

Raven and Lady of the Lake were converted from steam in the 1930s.

Lady of the Lake was launched on 26 June, 1877 and is believed to be the oldest working passenger vessel in the world.

Raven was commissioned after the tour operator Thomas Cook suggested a second boat was needed in peak holiday season. It was built on the Clyde and delivered in parts by train to Penrith, then transported by horse and cart to Pooley Bridge and assembled on the lakeside. It made its maiden voyage in 1889.

Above: **Lady of the Lake.**

Lady Dorothy, originally a seagoing vessel from Guernsey, joined the fleet in 2001.

Lady Wakefield was built in 1949, fully restored, and renamed by HRH Princess Alexandra in 2007.

Finally, Western Belle was built in 1935. After working on the Rivers Tamar, Yealm and Thames, she was refurbished and launched on Ullswater in 2011.

▼ Lady of the Lake has led a colourful life. In 1881 she sank at her moorings at Pooley Bridge, engulfed by large waves in rough weather. She sank again at the same mooring during a storm in 1958. The local fire brigade refloated her – an event filmed by my father on his 9.5mm movie camera. The film is now in the Ullswater Steamers archive. In 1965 Lady was badly damaged by fire while on the slipway at Waterside and it was thought she would never sail again. She remained out of service for 14 years. After a restoration costing £70,000, Lady was relaunched in 1979 by local MP William Whitelaw, then Home Secretary.

STEAMERS

After hunting with the Ullswater Foxhounds in Martindale years ago, legendary huntsman Joe Bowman decided to return to Glenridding by steamer. On discovering that he would have to pay a fare for each hound he let them ashore at Howtown while he stayed on board.

As the boat progressed, Joe blew his hunting horn and the hounds trotted along the lakeside path to be reunited with him at their kennels above Patterdale.

In 1895 Raven was made a temporary royal yacht to mark the visit of the German Kaiser, Wilhelm II, to his friend Lord Lonsdale at Lowther Castle. Her decks were – inevitably – painted yellow for the occasion.

Below: **Raven at the Glenridding landing stage.**

PATTERDALE

Patterdale

Though almost seamlessly joined to Glenridding, Patterdale feels more of a real village than purely a walkers' hub / service station. I've always been fond of Patterdale, which seems to be set at an inappropriate part of the valley amongst craggy outcrops and pitted hillsides. However, built into the slopes and backed by trees and fells, the huddle of slate buildings is fascinating to draw.

Patterdale retains an old-fashioned air. The White Lion Inn, set at a bottleneck in the main road, is a popular (though not with motorists!) landmark and hostelry. Its shape, like the bows of a ship heading south, is odd, as the field behind it could easily have accommodated a square-shaped building.

Above: **The White Lion bottleneck with Angletarn Pikes on the horizon.**
Below: **Patterdale village.**

Patterdale's active fire station is a reminder that the village is still relatively inaccessible. A memorable callout was to MV Raven when she was filling with water and sinking at her moorings after a stopcock had failed. A fast pump-out averted potential calamity.

PATTERDALE

A favourite of many people (including a certain A. Wainwright), the Patterdale valley stretches for three glorious miles from Ullswater to Kirkstone Pass. A narrow band of farmland twists through an avenue of fells, while Goldrill Beck flows attractively out of Brothers Water and the A592 road winds through mixed woodland and pasture. There's a scattering of picturesque farms, and houses laden with flowers in summer.

As the only direct route between Ullswater and Windermere, Patterdale is busy with traffic all year round, but there's a quiet walking track along the east side of the valley with fine views of the dale, Ullswater and the Helvellyn range of fells.

Three smaller dales branch west off the main valley. Grisedale rises from the village of Patterdale to Grisedale Hause, climbing between Fairfield and Seat Sandal before descending to Grasmere, while Deepdale and Dovedale cut deep into the fells, each with a superb arrangement of crags at its head.

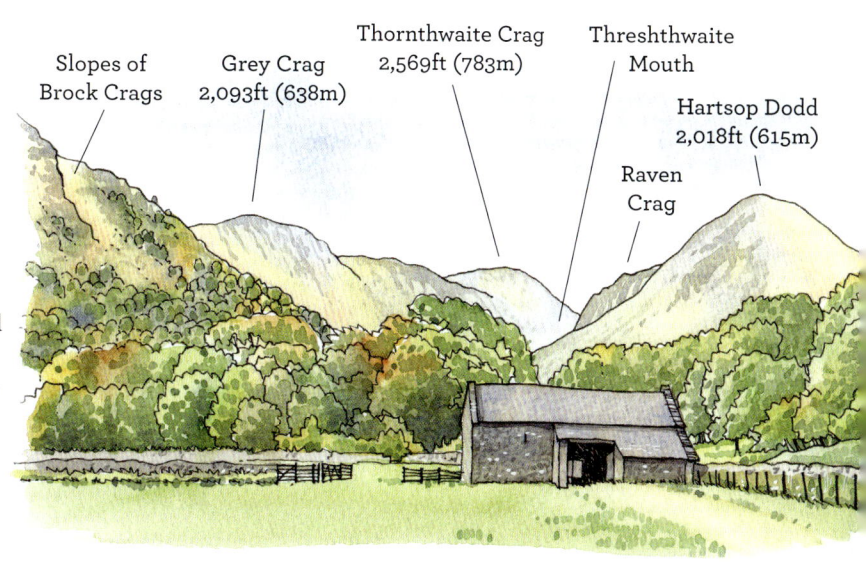

Patterdale is prone to flooding after heavy rain and was particularly badly hit by a huge downpour in November 2009 and by Storm Desmond in 2015.

Above: **Mid-Patterdale.**
Below: **Deepdale.**

HARTSOP

Hartsop

The delightful hamlet of Hartsop is snuggled between steep fells at the end of a cul-de-sac lane towards the south end of Patterdale. During the 14th century Hartsop was the biggest settlement and centre of industry in the valley. Renowned for wool spinning, it also had corn and cloth mills, with tailors, cobblers and blacksmiths looking after the needs of workers in the nearby lead mines.

Several houses in the rudimentary main street have galleries outside with carved oak balustrades and steps leading up to them. Usually referred to as 'spinning galleries', they were more likely used to *display* wool so dealers from Kendal could ride up and down the street sampling the goods.

Above: An old oven set in a wall, possibly to keep deliveries of milk cool.
Left: Low House Farm.

Hartsop is a marvellously chaotic jumble of tumbledown buildings, overgrown outhouses and enclosures, old gates, fences, dry-stone walls and farm implements. Tall trees overhang colourful gardens and noisy, tail-wagging sheepdogs come up close to be patted.

Pasture Beck runs alongside the village and once drove a mill on the hillside. Now, work done, the beck is a softly spoken watercourse crossed by an attractive packhorse bridge.

A few cottages look a little bit too neat – with the cultivated folksiness of potted plants, hanging baskets and green wellies in the doorway – but generally Hartsop remains an outdoor living museum of 17th-century Lakeland.

In a distance of little more than 300 yards the village has ten listed buildings. A finer collection of vernacular Lakeland architecture is hard to find.

I love it.

HARTSOP

Above left: **High Beckside.**
Above right: **Fell Yeat and the green lane.**
Below: **Cottage with a stepped 'spinning gallery'.**

Low House Farm at the entrance to the village is an outstanding example of a 17th-century Lakeland farmstead, where a barn and cattle shed were built on either end of the dwelling to help keep the human occupants warm. Fell Yeat was once the Bunch o' Birks Inn, set on a green lane used by packhorses; the lane still crosses the beck at a ford before winding its way to Kirkstone Pass.

A car park at the top of the village is a controversial modern intrusion, much derided by AW in his *Wainwright in the Valleys of Lakeland* book.

A rough track from the car park passes extensive sheep pens before heading up Hayeswater Gill into the High Street fells.

Hayeswater, a small lake above the valley, was dammed in 1908 and provided water for Penrith until 2005. In the summer of 2014 United Utilities removed the dam, returning the lake to its natural state. A new footbridge was built across Hayeswater Beck.

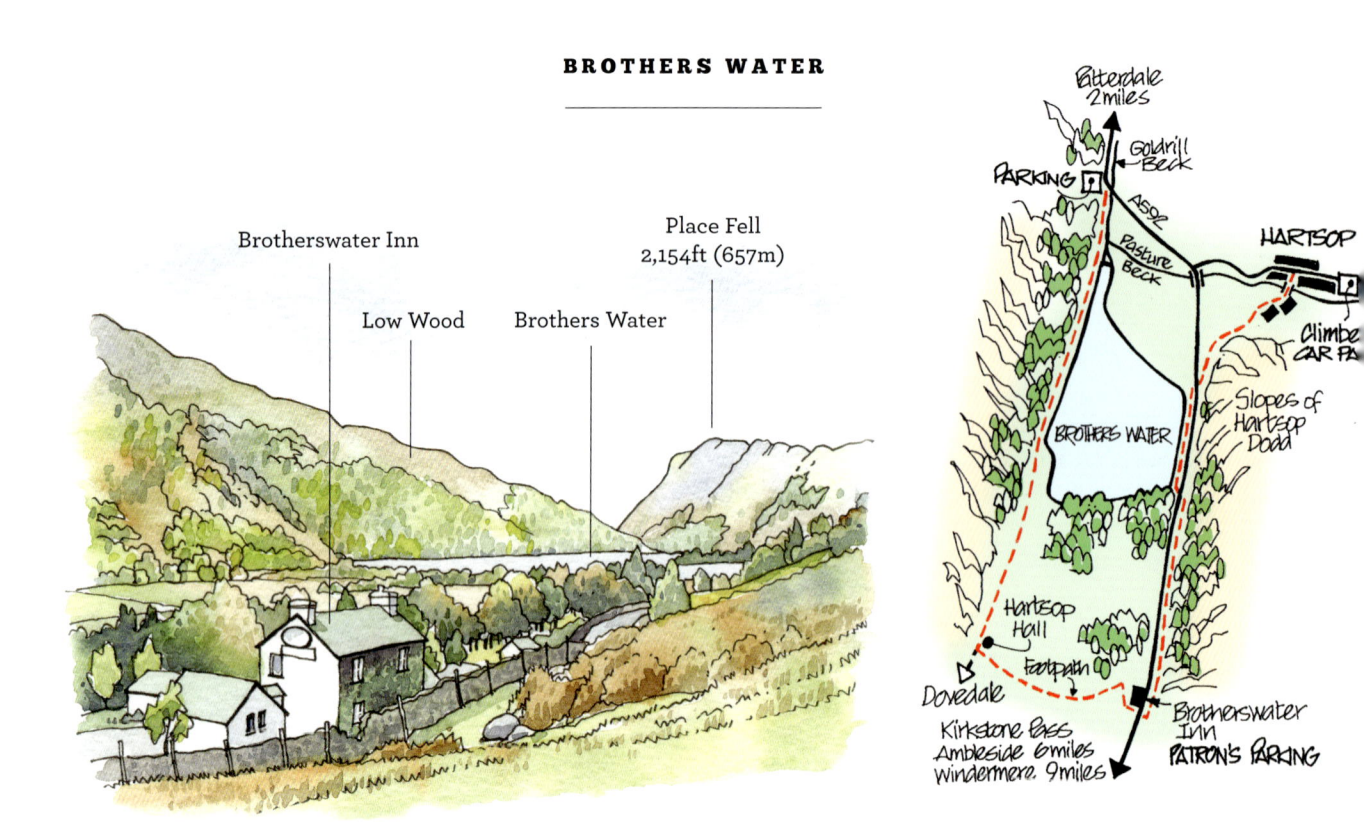

BROTHERS WATER

Brotherswater Inn
Low Wood
Place Fell
2,154ft (657m)
Brothers Water

Patterdale 2 miles
PARKING
Goldrill Beck
A592
Pasture Beck
HARTSOP
Climbers CAR PARK
Slopes of Hartsop Dodd
BROTHERS WATER
Hartsop Hall
Footpath
Dovedale
Kirkstone Pass
Ambleside 6 miles
Windermere 9 miles
Brotherswater Inn
PATRON'S PARKING

Brothers Water

The footprint of this curious, almost square-shaped lake almost fills the valley floor. Brothers Water is around half a mile in length, a quarter-mile across and has a depth of around 50ft at its southwest corner. The lake was originally called Broad Water and is said to have been changed to Brothers Water in the 18th century after two brothers drowned in it while skating.

More like a tarn than a lake, its picturesque qualities escape me, but it does make an excellent foreground for the magnificent view up-valley to Dovedale. On a practical level it also provides a holding point for the colossal amount of water that flows off the surrounding mountains and regularly floods Patterdale.

Dovedale is a short valley with, at its head, one of Lakeland's most fabulous collections of crags rising dramatically from coppiced woodland. It's a playground for serious rock climbers and out of bounds to mere mortals like me, who prefer to admire the panorama

Kirkstone Pass
Red Screes 2,541ft (775m)
Middle Dodd 2,106ft (642m)
Caiston Gill

40

BROTHERS WATER

from the comfort of the Brotherswater Inn terrace.

An excellent family walk goes around the lake, taking in Hartsop with a pit stop at the Inn.

Across the valley, 16th-century Hartsop Hall was formerly home of the de Lancasters family, who passed it on to Sir John Lowther, one-time Lord Lonsdale. After that it became an ordinary farmhouse.

Local legend has it that when the hall was extended in the 18th century, it was built across an ancient right-of-way. A number of dalesmen insisted on their rights and defiantly walked through the new extension.

If true, this was possibly the first mass trespass – a century before the famous one on Kinder Scout, Derbyshire, in 1932.

Left: Hartsop Hall.
Below: Dovedale from the Brotherswater Inn.

High Hartsop Dodd 1,703ft (519m)
Little Hart Crag 2,091ft (637m)
Hogget Gill
Dovedale
Dove Crag 2,603ft (792m)
The Strangs
Hart Crag 2,698ft (822m)
Fairfield 2,863ft (873m)
Slopes of Hartsop above How

Threlkeld

Drainpipes, Cydrax and t' crack

Four miles from Keswick and 15 from Penrith, Threlkeld is wonderfully set in a broad valley between Blencathra to the north and Clough Head to the south. St John's in the Vale, an exquisite little valley with a twinkling, tree-lined river and tremendous rock-strewn cliffs, branches off south, while low hills at Burns shut off the valley from Keswick.

An east wind often blows across open Troutbeck Moor, giving the village a cold and blustery climate. Keswick folk describe Threlkeld as an 'extra coat' place.

The busy A66 bypasses the main village, which follows the twisting old road across the

Below: Blencathra, the Public Room and the former petrol station, 'Cappies' (right) – now a private house.

THRELKELD

lower slopes of Gategill Fell, central bastion of mighty Blencathra. The other part of the village lies across the valley on the slopes of Threlkeld Knotts. Quarrying began here in the 1870s and continued until 1982. The granite was used for railway ballast, road kerbs and in Thirlmere dam. Initial output was a few hundred tons a year, but by 1894 it had risen to 80,000 tons. Terraced houses were built for the workers, with Threlkeld railway station nearby.

We moved into a new council house at Threlkeld in 1952, initially receiving a tepid welcome from the villagers; we were incomers, after all, from Westmorland – another county. However, we were soon accepted and became part of a vibrant and supportive community. It was a huge lifestyle change for all of us, and there were even children of my own age – lots of them – something I'd never enjoyed at Pooley Bridge.

Our house on Ghyll Bank was one of a dozen semis built on the lower slopes of Blencathra. It seemed vast, with three bedrooms, a bathroom, living room, sitting room, kitchen and washhouse. I started at the local school, my father ran an upholstery workshop in Keswick and my mother enjoyed her new domain with my two brothers, then aged three and four.

Gategill mine on Blencathra was worked for lead and zinc between 1661 and 1928. At the turn of the century 100 local men were employed there and Threlkeld enjoyed a spectacular – if short-lived – boom. Terraced houses in the village were built using waste from the mine.

Mining over a number of years caused considerable heavy metal pollution in the area. We used to race bikes – cobbled together from parts found in the village rubbish dump – over the extensive waste tips. They've now been removed, the site cleaned up and our bikes returned to the tip.

Below: **Blease Road (commonly 'T' Sanny Road' or 'Duck Street') climbs out of the village to the Blencathra Outdoor Activity Centre, once a TB isolation hospital.**

In the late 1950s Threlkeld had...
- Four shops
- Two pubs
- A post office
- A petrol filling station
- A railway station
- A school
- Evening classes
- A village policeman
- A resident nurse
- A tailors
- A joiner and undertaker
- A butcher
- A cobbler
- Scout, Cub and Brownie packs
- A church
- A public room
- A tea garden
- BATS theatre group
- A youth club
- A daily and evening newspaper delivery
- Cricket and football clubs
- An annual village trip to Morecambe.

THRELKELD

When I lived in Threlkeld the Horse & Farrier was at the centre of village life. It's one of the oldest pubs in Cumbria and has the inscription 'CIG 1688' on the lintel over the front door. The initials are those of Christopher and Grace Irton, then living at Threlkeld Hall.

The nearby Salutation Inn is even older – a former coaching inn dating to 1664. Now under the same management, both are smart gastropubs with rooms to let.

Fox hunting in the Lake District used to be hugely popular, with reports of the chase in local papers like football matches. The opening hunt of the season started outside the Farrier in October with 'stirrup cups' – an alcoholic bracer – for participants.

Hunting on the Lakeland fells was different to the 'polite' social occasions in the south. Only the huntsman and the dog whipper-in wore red coats, and no horses were involved. Lakeland farmers hunted to keep the number of foxes down – and they did it on foot.

The Blencathra Foxhounds, kennelled locally at Gategill, were reckoned to be the best in the business, hunting across Thirlmere, Derwent Water, Skiddaw and Caldbeck district. The first kill of the opening hunt on Blencathra was brought back to the Farrier and hung on a nail banged into the front door.

Arguments over the barbarity of hunting with dogs mostly ended when it was banned in 2004. I've seen a fox being torn to pieces by hounds – and the result of a fox getting into a hen house; neither was a pretty sight.

On the fifth Sunday in Lent the Horse & Farrier used to celebrate 'Carlin Sunday', or Passion Sunday, by cooking big pans of carlins for distribution to the villagers. Carlins are small dried peas that were soaked in water overnight then boiled until tender. My mother used to send me down to the pub with a big jug to fill. I used to love them – and a local rude rhyme paid tribute to their effectiveness as a laxative.

▲ The Farrier prepared half-time coffee for the Threlkeld football team – with a brandy booster. The pitch was a good way from the pub, so I was one of the volunteers who jostled to collect the coffee urn and cups – and test the potent brew on the way back. If the team was two goals down, the landlord usually upped the brandy content; I don't know if it ever improved the results, but nobody complained.

Right: **The Sally (Salutation Inn).**

THRELKELD

▲ I liked Threlkeld school. The teachers were a friendly bunch who somehow managed to get me through the 11-plus exam for entry to Keswick Grammar School. For me and a number of pals from the village, going to 'the big school' was a new and exciting prospect.

▲ St Mary's Church, built in 1777, is stark and simple, with a squat bell tower that is a remnant of an earlier thatched structure. In an old village ritual, the churchyard gates are tied shut during weddings and not reopened until the bridegroom throws coins for local children to scramble for.

Hound trails were regularly held on the quarry side of the valley and are still popular throughout Cumbria.

A trail of up to ten miles long is set by a 'trailer' dragging a bundle of rags soaked in paraffin and aniseed. The hounds then follow the trail around the hills for half an hour or so. When spotted approaching the finish line the hounds' owners shout, whistle and wave, trying to attract their dog home first.

It's a great spectacle, but the main attraction has always been the betting, with on-field bookies shouting the odds and winning dogs being rewarded with prime steak and - it's rumoured - champagne.

Back at our new home, my mother celebrated having a kitchen by holding regular baking days. Apple pasties, gingerbread, biscuits, cheese straws, shortbread, scones, sponge cakes and more were all turned out for our delectation.

Main meals improved too, with chips accompanying pretty much everything (father would eat anything with chips). We always had HP brown sauce; there was none of that tomato stuff on our table. I spent mealtimes trying to understand the French blurb on the side of the sauce bottle – without much luck.

My favourite meal was Tattie Pot, which consisted of cheap meat, black pudding, dripping, lots of potatoes, onions and anything my mother wanted to get rid of. Simmered for ages in the oven, it tasted wonderful and would tolerate a few days of being reheated, the flavour improving each time. Many northern families lived on Tattie Pot and to this day many Lakeland pubs hold Tattie Pot nights.

Grandad Watson came to live with us for a while. After he died, I altered his over-sized sports jacket and made myself a passable teddy boy drape.

I also began to taper my trousers to drainpipe proportions, using one of my father's old sewing machines.

The results were variable. Who would have thought getting the same taper in each leg would be so difficult? Certainly not me.

A large quiff was also *de rigueur* at the time. I discovered that a mix of sugar and water made an excellent and cheap hair gel. Sadly, after stepping outside into the hostile Threlkeld wind, my fabulous quiff never survived for long.

THRELKELD

One day in the early 1950s three of us piled off the school bus anxious to see what was going on at Taylor's Cottages. A man on the roof was manipulating a large, metal bar construction on a pole attached to the chimney. A cable ran down the roof and into the living room. The owner of the house kept coming out, waving his arms and barking instructions: "Roond a bit... whooa... back a bit... more... la'al bit... no, t'uther way... hod it theeer... reet... no... oh, start agin...!"

We peered through the window at what looked like a tall wooden box on end. A postcard-size section at the top showed a snow storm in flickering light. At the owner's invitation we were led into the darkened room. After further bellowed instructions, the snowstorm cleared slightly to reveal a stringed puppet.

"Muffin the Mule!" exclaimed the proud owner, thumbs hooked behind his braces: "Television! Whot d'y' recken?"

Above: 17th-century Taylor's Cottages, now mostly holiday lets.

Our response was "Aye, au reet," but once outside, our joint opinion was: "If that's television it'll niver catch on."

Threlkeld was a congenial place. Everyone knew everyone else and considered they knew everything about everyone else. If you did something at one end of the village it was said the other end would know about it before you could walk there.

'T' crack' was a mainstay of village life. On sunny days old ladies would sit at their open front doors eager to chat with anyone passing. Cappie's petrol station beside the public room was a popular (though not always with Cappie) gathering place at the weekends, where gossip was exchanged and repartee was rife. You were expected to come up with a quick, witty comment or reply to anything said. Passers-by on an afternoon walk would join in, with women as sharp as the men.

Threlkeld cricket field is overlooked by a bank of rocks with a culvert across the top – once a drain from the mine. It's a perfect place to build a rocky seat to watch the game. It was also a hotbed of banter, wisecracks and forensic analysis of what the team was doing wrong on the pitch. Banter goes on in most close communities and helps bind them together. After a professional lifetime of writing gags and striving to make people laugh I consider my growing up and learning the ropes in Threlkeld to have been an invaluable grounding.

Since opening in 1901, the public room (now the Village Hall) has been a hub of village activity. Dances, bring-and-buy sales, whist drives, WI meetings and children's Christmas parties were standard events.

We also enjoyed concerts with humorous tales told in local dialect, amateur magicians, pub singers and novelty acts, including one where a man in evening dress played a saw like a violin, and a musical turn from the locally famous Crosthwaite Bell Ringers. The big attraction for us lads was when local girls donned short skirts and tap danced.

Blencathra Amateur Theatrical Society (BATS) put on plays, both drama and comedy, to packed houses. Villagers would take on surprising new personalities, with the dourest of farmers bringing the house down with an appearance in one of the comedy 'Whitehall Farces'.

Hunt Balls with accordion bands were also memorable – typically after the pubs shut. Too young to be served, we started supping Cydrax before dances. Then, after various 'drunken' antics, we made the shocking discovery that Cyrdax was actually non-alcoholic.

By the late 1950s rock and roll was beginning to be heard in our part of the outback, so we organised a youth club in the public room where we could play records and jive – Cydrax-free.

After more than 100 years of heavy village use, the public room was showing its age. Thanks mainly to National Lottery funding a complete renovation was undertaken. With an excellent coffee shop added, the revitalised public room reopened as the Village Hall in 2014. Profit from the community-owned coffee shop helps fund the Hall and its maintenance.

There were always odd jobs around the village that allowed an enterprising young lad to top up his pocket money.

I'd deliver telegrams from the post office to outlying hamlets, help the milkman with his deliveries or assist my pal Tommy on his evening paper round.

Collecting the daily papers from the railway station was a delicate operation on a bike. I used to balance the heavy bag on my handlebars, but if it fell off onto the front wheel the strap would drag me over the bars.

I helped out with seasonal jobs on the farms. Picking potatoes at the end of the summer holidays was back-breaking but profitable work. Farmers were notoriously tight with money, but you'd get fantastic meals out in the fields by way of compensation.

My favourite job was 'gardening' for a lovely old lady on the village outskirts. It involved no more than mowing her lawn and light weeding, but she always paid well and brought out a wonderful afternoon tea on a tray. I think she enjoyed the company more than my green-fingered expertise.

Above: One of the old village shops, now a holiday let.

> **After various drunken antics we made the shocking discovery that Cydrax was actually non-alcoholic.**

THRELKELD

Threlkeld's annual sheepdog trials were held on the field opposite Church Row. Each trial began with five sheep being released at one end of the field with the shepherd and dog at the other. The dog was then sent to gather the sheep and return them through a series of obstacles controlled by whistles and calls from the shepherd. Tension mounted at the climax when the sheep had to be penned.

Normally the trials were a monumentally boring day out. One year, however, the proceedings were considerably enlivened when a cow in the next field began to calve. Loud bellowing alerted the farmer and helpers flooded out of the beer tent. Various arms were stuck up the cow's rear end, and with the assistance of a rope the calf was eventually delivered safely.

The farmer and helpers bowed to their biggest audience for a cow giving birth, before returning to the beer tent for revivers.

Above: Church Row in 1985. On the left is the joiner's shop, dating to the 1500s. It is thought to be the oldest building in the village.
Below: The Old Joiner's Shop in 2020.

According to the Lake District National Park Authority a town or village with 10% or more second and/or holiday homes is unsustainable. Central government puts the figure at 20%. By 2011 Threlkeld had reached 24.1%. Local people are being priced out of houses – yet depend on tourism for their livelihood. Achieving a balance is almost impossible, and the problem is getting worse.

THRELKELD

The stone Threlkeld Bridge on the A594 old road at the village outskirts has been described as 'the bridge over three rivers' as two, St John's Beck and the Glenderamackin, merge under the arches to form the Greta.

St John's Beck meanders out of Thirlmere along lovely St John's in the Vale. One of our favourite bathing places was on a sweeping bend near the bridge. With a group of pals I spent many a blissful summer afternoon jumping into the cool water and lounging on the bank chatting to girls.

Later we'd wander back into the village for refreshment at Beckside Tea Gardens. I'd have a dollop of ice cream in a glass with Vimto poured over it. I can still taste it now.

> **I spent many a blissful summer afternoon jumping in the cool water and lounging on the bank chatting to girls.**

The River Glenderamackin rises on Blencathra near Sharp Edge and Scales Tarn. It flows north around Souther Fell before turning south through Mungrisdale and then west along the valley bottom to Threlkeld, where it regularly floods.

Bridgend, an ancient farmstead near the cricket field, is nicknamed 'Noah's Ark' locally as it's often surrounded by floodwater.

The splendid Celtic name of the river dates back to the tenth century when Norse invaders joined the Celts, who were living below Threlkeld Knotts, to establish a new settlement across the river, calling it *Thrall's Spring* – Threlkeld.

Below: **Threlkeld Bridge.**

THRELKELD

The River Greta valley, with its winding river and abundance of trees climbing up the hillsides, is one of Lakeland's most picturesque and precious areas – breathtaking in autumn colours. I used to enjoy walking from Threlkeld to Keswick through Brundholme Wood across the flank of Latrigg, then returning home on the bus. That way I could have a look at both sides of the valley.

From 1865 to 1972 a single track of the Penrith to Cockermouth railway ran through the Greta valley, providing Keswick with a memorable entrance for visitors. A long tunnel at Briery on the outskirts brought them into the station.

We used to roam freely in the woods around the Greta, building huts, climbing trees and mucking about in traditional teenage boy-fashion. A popular pastime was placing copper half pennies on the train line then marvelling at their transformation into oversized and extremely thin 'pennies' after a train had rumbled over them.

Some summers we'd build rafts to float on the Greta. 'Float' was the theory, anyway. In reality they fell to bits soon after being launched. The most satisfying part of the adventure was collecting materials – old oil drums, discarded doors, planks – and tying them together with string, rope and wire. It kept us busy for weeks.

When I was a kid, I wore wellies nearly all the time. After any activity involving water I'd go home with at least one 'soaker'. My wellies would then be stuffed with pages of the *Daily Mirror* to dry out, and my socks were hung from the mantelpiece over the fire. There they would gently steam until my mother ran out of patience, wallpaper began to curl off the walls... and the budgie fell off his perch.

THRELKELD

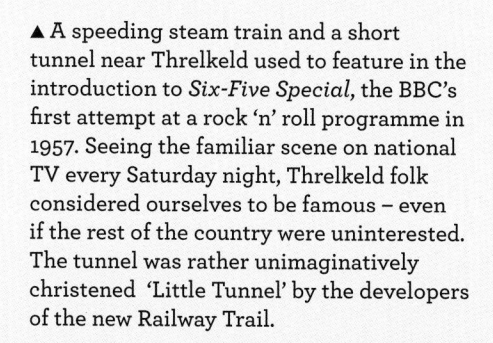

▲ A speeding steam train and a short tunnel near Threlkeld used to feature in the introduction to *Six-Five Special*, the BBC's first attempt at a rock 'n' roll programme in 1957. Seeing the familiar scene on national TV every Saturday night, Threlkeld folk considered ourselves to be famous – even if the rest of the country were uninterested. The tunnel was rather unimaginatively christened 'Little Tunnel' by the developers of the new Railway Trail.

▲ Between Threlkeld and Keswick stations, the railway line crosses the Greta eight times in less than four miles. When the line was removed, the route became a popular footpath between Threlkeld and Keswick, with the iconic bridges remaining a feature. They are of bow-string girder construction with various sizes and alignments. On some the bow is on the top; on others it is underneath. In 2015 Storm Desmond turned the Greta into a devastating torrent. Bridges were swept away and others badly damaged. After years of temporary repairs, a £7.9 million package from various sources enabled the route to be reconstructed and rebranded as the Keswick to Threlkeld Railway Trail. It was reopened in 2020.

Below: Blencathra and the Glenderamackin valley from Burns Brow.

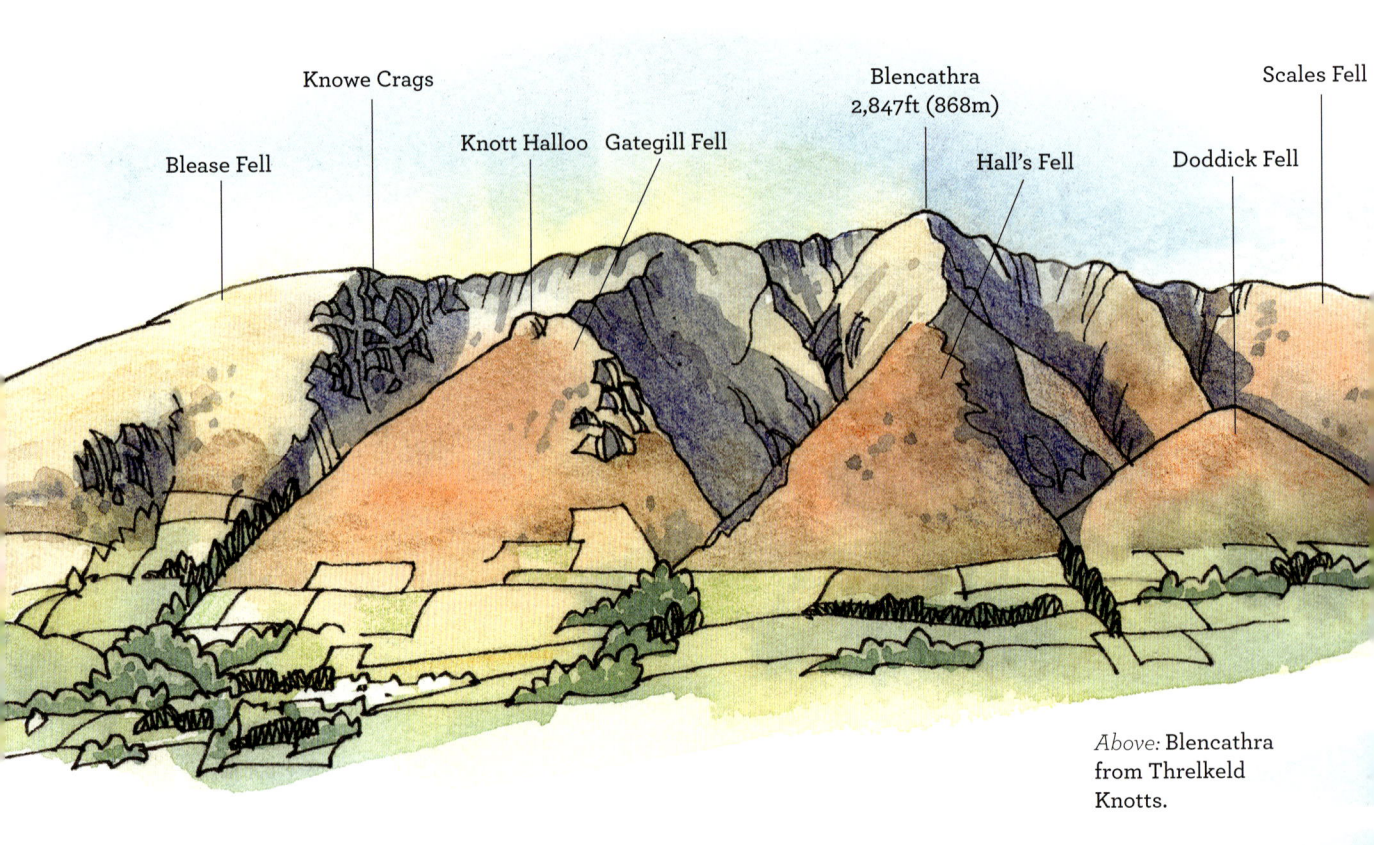

THRELKELD

Blease Fell · Knowe Crags · Knott Halloo · Gategill Fell · Blencathra 2,847ft (868m) · Hall's Fell · Doddick Fell · Scales Fell

Above: Blencathra from Threlkeld Knotts.

Blencathra

My first mountain epiphany occurred when I was about eight years old and on a train from Penrith to Keswick Bank Holiday Sports with my father. Beyond Penruddock station the train passed through a cutting then suddenly burst onto the open fellside – a perfect viewpoint for the grandeur of Blencathra across the valley. Used to the benign hills around Pooley Bridge, I had never seen a mountain that looked so awesome and yet so beautiful. It was unimaginable then that two years later I would live at its foot.

We called it Saddleback. Everyone in the village did. Blencathra was the visitors' name. We thought climbers were a bit odd, travelling all the way to Threlkeld just to climb Saddleback; few villagers ever did.

I've never thought of Blencathra as a challenge to conquer; rather the opposite.

Like the bridge at Pooley Bridge it has been a friend – a sanctuary from challenges elsewhere. I loved to sit on the slopes of Gategill Fell looking across the village to St John's and Helvellyn, marvelling at the peaceful perfection.

The glory of Blencathra lies in its trio of spurs – narrow ridges that leave the shattered scree of the main mountain, spreading to form substantial buttresses that drop into the fields of the valley. Between the spurs are rocky ravines, each with a beck, each a delight for a fraught teenager to explore.

As Blencathra's north side is generally dismissed as being boggy and boring, Mother Nature was bountiful in presenting the mountain's most dramatic side to the world at large. In addition, she was clever enough to keep the mountain's most iconic ridge – Sharp Edge – hidden from the valley.

THRELKELD

I've never crossed Sharp Edge. I've been to look at it a few times. On each occasion I went no further – the view itself was scary enough.

Climbing steeply to Foule Crag, Sharp Edge is the shortest of Blencathra's ridges, but it is naked rock with a serrated edge that lives up to its name. Despite a fearsome aspect, it receives a constant stream of walkers lured by its airy reputation.

Some 900ft below its crest lie the dark waters of Scales Tarn, so hemmed in by high crags it's almost always in shadow. Years ago the locals believed it was so dark that even at midday you could see stars reflected in its surface.

Below: **Evening shadows on Blencathra from below Scales.**

Walking along the familiar old road through Threlkeld these days is a sad experience for me. I'm always struck by how quiet it is and how few people are out on the streets. They all seem to have disappeared – along with the shops. I suppose I'm a visitor now, so I try to look at Threlkeld as a newcomer, but thoughts from 60 years ago flood back. Even dear old Blencathra seems overrun. The vibrant community I recall with so much affection has long gone. Us old'uns will forever mourn its passing. However, I also treasure my memories of growing up in the village. And whatever happens to it, *my* beloved Blencathra – Saddleback – will never change.

Keswick

School, starry nights and itchy feet

The old market town of Keswick, with its tightly packed slate buildings, is fabulously set between Derwent Water and Skiddaw, with Borrowdale and the high fells stretching away south.

According to legend, in AD550 Saint Kentigern preached at Crosthwaite, where a church was eventually built in 1181. Worshippers from the valleys started holding unofficial markets after services, much to the annoyance of neighbouring Cockermouth, which held a royal charter for its market.

After years of complaints about illegal competition, Edward I finally settled the squabble by awarding a new market charter to a small cheese dairy south of the River Greta. This grew to become the town of Keswick, leaving St Kentigern's Church isolated at Crosthwaite to this day.

The local mining industry was a haphazard business until a 1564 decree by Elizabeth I brought skilled miners from Germany to win copper ore from Newlands and Borrowdale.

Treated with suspicion by the natives, some set up home on Derwent Island. It has been suggested that they introduced the famous Cumberland sausage to the region – but don't mention that anywhere near a local butcher. A large smelter was built at Brigham where the A66 road bridge now crosses the Greta.

The town enjoyed a century of prosperity until the English Civil War, when Cromwell's troops destroyed the smelter, and with it the Keswick copper industry.

By the mid-18th century the Lake Poets' evocative descriptions were attracting affluent visitors to the area, but it was the opening of the railway in 1864 that supersized the tourist onslaught. Keswick soon had the most bed and breakfast accommodation of any town in Cumbria. Today, numerous holiday lets, second homes and caravan and camping sites have added to the tally.

The town absorbs a vast, ever-changing procession of visitors and, less successfully, their cars, SUVs, motorhomes... and dogs.

Left: The town's oldest building, St Kentigern's Church, mainly 14th-century with earlier church foundations.

▲ Keswick's iconic Moot Hall was built in 1813 and has been used as a courthouse, market, prison, museum and town hall. An unusual one-handed clock in the tower marks the hour with a mournful toll of its original 17th-century curfew bell.

For many years the building was rendered in black and white, the render controversially removed in a 1975 renovation. The ground floor used to be open, and I remember local lads on bikes using it as a race track when it was raining outside. Since 1971, it has housed a National Park information bureau, said to be the busiest in Lakeland. In 2018 Allerdale Borough Council sold the much-loved Moot Hall to the Battersby Hall Trust, a local charity, with the buyers pledging it would remain a building for community use.

KESWICK

Above: **Lower Main Street.**

KESWICK

For over 700 years a market has been held in Market Place, now every Thursday and Saturday. A wide range of local products and food is sold, including artisan cheeses, Herdwick sheep fleeces and designer woolly jumpers.

Keswick now depends almost entirely on tourism, and most of the retail premises in the town are outdoor equipment stores or gift shops, alongside an abundance of hospitality outlets. Since Market Place was pedestrianised, cafés and pubs have moved tables outside, giving the area an agreeable social atmosphere.

The large chain stores are mainly absent and many businesses are locally owned, which enables Keswick to maintain its reputation as the lively, hardworking and homely place that I remember so well.

▲ Flooding has long been a problem at High Hill, where the Greta flows around the former pencil mill and under Greta Bridge. A medieval bridge once crossed here on the main coach road from Kendal to Cockermouth. The present two-arched bridge (*above*) was built in 1926. In 2015 floodwater rose to the top of the bridge walls.

▲ Pencils have been made at Keswick since the 1500s using plumbago (graphite) mined in Borrowdale. Originally a cottage industry, manufacture expanded in 1832 when the first custom-built factory was opened, becoming the Cumberland Pencil Company in 1916. Construction was started in the 1920s and completed in 1950. It closed in 2007 when production moved to Workington.

Waste pencils were piled on a heap next to Keswick School field before being burnt. My pal Chas, who knew everyone who worked in the mill, regularly 'arranged' for discarded pencils to fall our way. There was usually not much wrong with them and I was never without a selection of colour pencils to draw with.

The Pencil Museum, located on the site of the original factory, is nowadays a tourist attraction, partly due to its housing the world's longest colour pencil, which is almost 26ft long, and yellow.

KESWICK

Above: **The Moot Hall,** upper Market Place and Lake Road.

KESWICK

▲ The former police station and magistrates' court in Bank Street was built in 1902 and is now Grade II listed. The gabled wing of the courtroom features a Venetian window, and a single column supports a segmented pediment over the formidable entrance. In 2014 the building was converted to a Wetherspoons pub with the wonderful name 'The Chief Justice of the Common Pleas'.

This commemorates Sir John Bankes, a leading Royalist during the English Civil War, who was born at Castlerigg near Keswick in 1589. He became Charles I's Attorney General and Chief Justice of the Common Pleas, which relates to common law created by judges.

A slightly less impressive commemoration to Sir John is a bust in Upper Fitz Park, close to the museum.

Right: **The Wild Strawberry in Main Street, one of the town's oldest and most characterful buildings.**

KESWICK

With up-market gift shops, restaurants, cafés, bistros, bars and pubs, Lake Road is one of Keswick's busiest tourist streets. A 12ft-tall metal giraffe outside the Treeby & Bolton store was made of recycled oil drums by a team of ten artists in Kenya and shipped here in a giant container. Apart from the popular sculpture, Treeby & Bolton also boasts a fashionable shop, gallery and café.

George Fisher opened in 1957, when it was the first business to import mountain equipment from Austria. Since then it has become one of the busiest outdoors stores in the Lakes.

Nearby is the Wainwright Inn, a popular walkers' pub and shrine to the revered fell-walker, writer and artist, with a photo of AW and prints of his drawings across the walls. Wainwright was the son of an alcoholic and disliked pubs, so I sometimes wonder what he would have made of the widespread use of his name for pubs, bars and beers throughout the Lake District.

Above: **Lake Road.**
Left: **Treeby & Bolton.**

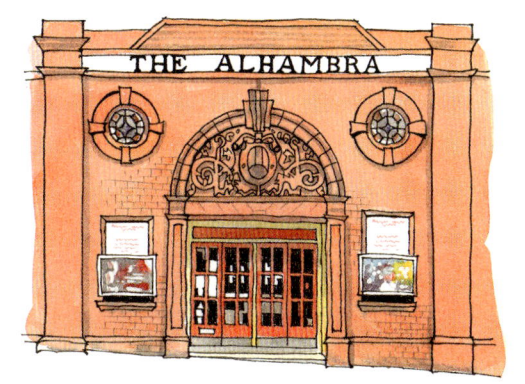

KESWICK

▲ The Alhambra cinema in St John's Street is an old-school, theatre-style picture house with a balcony and a mixed programme of mainstream blockbusters and indie productions. Built in 1913, it is one of the few UK cinemas to have been in continuous use for over 100 years. The ornate façade is the only red brick building in town.

Over the years the technical equipment has been regularly updated, with a switch from 35mm film to digital in 2018. A year later a successful crowd-funding campaign enabled the auditorium to be restored to its former glory.

In October 2021 work was completed on its latest redevelopment, which created a bar and a second, smaller screen.

The cinema was a significant part of my teenage life. At first, I sat in the front rows with a gang of pals, where we chatted and made fun of the films.

Later, if you copped off with a girl you advanced to a 'chummie' double seat in the back row – and whatever was on screen became of minor importance.

Serious film buffs sat in the circle with the old folks.

> **If you copped off with a girl you advanced to a 'chummie' double seat in the back row.**

▼ The Dog & Gun is one of Keswick's most popular hostelries, dating to the 18th century and Grade II listed.

A distinctive white stuccoed building with black quoins, its three-storey section towers above Lake Road just off the Market Square. The pub's signature dish is Hungarian Goulash, originating in medieval Hungary and cooked here for more than 60 years.

KESWICK

▶ Opened in 1999, the Theatre by the Lake replaced the Blue Box – a mobile theatre created after World War Two to take plays to places with no active theatres.

Situated at the end of Lake Road, and just yards from the lake, the theatre was the first to be built with the help of National Lottery funding. Its two stages host a full programme of drama, concerts, exhibitions, readings and talks. With high production values, the theatre is credited with turning Keswick into the main cultural centre of the north Lakes.

▼ Hope Park on Lake Road was donated to the town in 1974 by local dignitary Sir Percy Hope, a partner in the architectural practice which employed me for a while. I remember him as an imposing country gent dressed in a tweed suit with plus-four trousers. He always carried a shepherd's crook – even to the office.

During the 1920s the area was grazed by horses that transported coachloads of passengers from the station to their hotels. Sir Percy subsequently developed it into a miniature golf course, opened in 1927 by then British champion golfer J. H. Taylor. The ornamental garden was the private garden of Lady Hope.

> **Sir Percy always carried a shepherd's crook – even to the office.**

Below: Hope Park, St John's Church and distant Clough Head.

KESWICK

Above: **Keswick School in 1960.**

Keswick School

I was a pupil at Keswick School for five years, where I somehow managed to scrape together five GCE 'O' levels despite my lackadaisical efforts.

The co-educational grammar school included boarders, with some girls living in nearby Greta Hall – once home of Lake Poets Coleridge and Southey.

The school regime was based on that of an English private school, which is to say: Latin taught; rugger played; strict uniform (with cap) worn; homework and detention set; towels flicked in cold showers; and teachers dressed in flowing black robes. Bullying of first year pupils was a right of passage.

Intimidation I could cope with, but my first days were marked by getting lost between lessons and bewilderment at the range of facililites available – something I'd never experienced before.

We had chemistry, physics, biology and geography labs; a gym, a library, woodwork and art workshops; cloakrooms and showers; a refectory and a row of classrooms stretching almost to Stanger Street.

In 1997, Rawnsley Hall, part of the town school site, was sold to Keswick Ministries, an evangelical Christian organisation that runs the Keswick Convention, an annual three-week gathering of worship, preaching and bible study held in the town during July and August. Keswick Ministries also acquired the former pencil mill building as its headquarters in 2015.

The area around Rawnsley Hall has now suffered the fate of most open land in central Keswick – it's a car park.

Bottles of milk were handed out at morning break, with boarders also given a slice of bread and butter. They inevitably breakfasted far better than us day pupils, so breaktime would become a period of pleading and bartering over slices of white bread.

Outdoor activities and sport were high on the curriculum, with regular winter cross-country runs across the lower slopes of Latrigg and rugby played on half-flooded pitches beside the lake.

Between asthma attacks I was a decent sprinter and ran in 100 and 200-yard events and relays for the school. It came as a big surprise – not least to me – when I was awarded my athletics colours, which entitled me to wear a purple blazer in the summer term rather than regulation green.

Keswick School was founded in 1898, with the Rev. Cecil Grant, a pioneer of co-education, as headmaster. He also wrote the school song, *Assurgit Skidda Stabilis* – naturally in Latin. In 1980, the school merged with a comprehensive at Laithwaite on the edge of town, which gradually became the main school and was granted academy status in 2012.

Sports

Predictably, Station Road leads to the former station, lamentably closed since 1972. I was one of the scruffy urchins who greeted visitors arriving by train. We made easy pocket money ferrying luggage to hotels on home-made carts.

Fitz Park straddles the road, separating it into Upper and Lower parts. Upper Fitz Park is largely formal, with landscaped gardens and an arboretum with specimen trees and shrubs. The lower part is more open, with a children's playground and a multi-use football and basketball area. In 2001 *Wisden* voted Fitz Park the most beautiful cricket ground in England.

During the 1950s Lower Fitz Park hosted the Keswick Sports, held each August Bank Holiday, where huge crowds gathered to watch grass track cycle races and running events, along with fell races and the local speciality: Cumberland and Westmorland wrestling.

While still at school I ran in one of the 100-yard sprint heats, a handicapped event. I was given a 10-yard start as no-one knew, including me, how good or bad I was. My Uncle Billy, who ran a cycle and sports shop in Penrith, had given me a pair of running spikes and I was eager to try them out against the Flimby Flyer, who was favourite to win the event and starting off scratch.

After a good start I relaxed around the 98-yard point thinking I had the race won, which allowed the Flyer to steam past and take the tape. It was a disappointment, but I was gratified to receive a mouthful of abuse from the Flyer, who considered it a bit much that I had forced him to run harder than he'd planned for or expected.

Returning to school after the Bank Holiday break, I was summoned to the headmaster's study for a dressing down. I'd competed in a professional sporting event, which could disqualify me from ever running as an amateur for the school. Nobody warned me. Now I was tainted. "Nobert a bit of fun, sir."

The men's fell race, a torturous climb to the 1,207ft-high summit of Latrigg followed by a mad dash down, was usually won by Caldbeck shepherd Bill Teasdale. A short, barrel-chested man dressed in what looked like an M&S vest, he bounded into the sports field with the band playing 'D'ye Ken John Peel?' and the crowd, including me, standing to welcome home their hero.

The cycling events attracted competitors from all over the country and rivalry with local riders was intense. The three Hendry brothers from Glasgow were formidable racers and reckoned to clean up most of the prize money. With fixed-wheel bikes, feet clamped to the pedals, and riders pushing each other and arguing, the races were exciting events. There were some alarming pile-ups, but being on grass, rarely any serious injuries. The hard men would simply wipe off the blood and be back competing later in the meeting.

Sadly, despite the appearance of sporting celebrities such as middle-distance runner Gordon Pirie and shot-putter Arthur Rowe, interest in the Keswick Sports waned. Some say it was because gambling was not allowed on the park and there were no hound trails. Whatever the reasons, after two wet years in the early 1960s the event quietly died off.

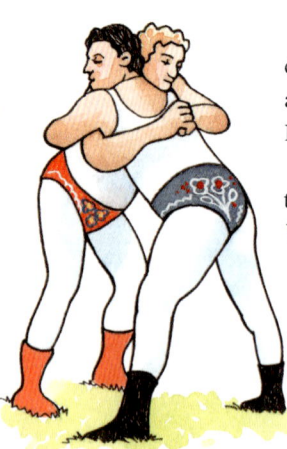

▲ A Cumberland and Westmorland wrestling bout starts with the two combatants facing each other, watched by two judges and a referee. After shaking hands they 'tak hod' – lock arms behind each others' back. The object is then to throw the other chap to the ground. If both fall over, the one on top wins.

As if that's not interesting enough, the two participants compete wearing old-fashioned long combinations with richly embroidered bathing trunks over them and socks, like characters in a Monty Python sketch.

Another great cultural centre in Station Street (at least for me) was the Pavilion, snuggled below the bridge at the riverside. When the pubs shut, we all crowded in for the Saturday night dance.

The band, a poker-faced group of middle-aged men in bowties and dinner jackets as worn as their repertoire, consisted of piano, drums and a small brass section, churning out a string of strict-tempo tunes for ballroom

KESWICK

▶ Keswick Museum stands on the edge of Lower Fitz Park, opened in a custom-built building during 1898 after 23 years in the Moot Hall. A complete restoration in 2013 added an extension and café overlooking the park. It boasts a collection of around 20,000 objects featuring the area's landscape, history and culture, including manuscripts from the Lakeland Poets and numerous oddities. The most famous exhibits are the Musical Stones (no, not *those* musical Stones) collected on Skiddaw by local stone mason Joseph Richardson in the 1830s. They sound in tune when struck and toured Victorian England as the 'Rock, Bell and Steel Band'.

◀ The old footbridge over the Greta into Upper Fitz Park was destroyed in the Storm Desmond floods when all kinds of debris (including a caravan) swept down the swollen river. A new all-metal bridge, 21 metres long and weighing more than 12 tons, was craned into position in 2017.

dancing. They only came marginally alive when playing what was ambitiously announced as 'a jive'.

I could usually cadge a lift home after the revelries, but on occasional clear nights I elected to forsake the usual ride in the back of a young farmer's van (where previous occupants could have been straw bales, turnips or sick sheep) and walked the four miles back to Threlkeld on my own.

Carried on an agreeable wave of beery contentment, I would walk the A66 beneath an enormous dome of dark sky packed with twinkling stars, the familiar silhouette of Saddleback guiding me home.

Opened in 1895, the Pavilion staged pantomimes, variety shows and dances, with a capacity for 1,400 people in the large hall and a stage big enough to accommodate 250 people.

It was demolished in 1987 and the site is now the YHA café.

KESWICK

▶ Rain and mist permitting, I had the pleasure of seeing the glorious panorama of Keswick and Newlands fells every day when going to school or work on the bus.

Freshly covered in snow on a winter's morning, the scene could be breathtaking. Low-lying mist would sometimes obscure the town, leaving the apparently untethered fells to float like ethereal icebergs in a deep blue sky. The spectacle was enough to silence cynical school children – and even move sleepy commuters to raise a heavy eyelid.

The view can also be a powerful distraction to motorists. Years later, when I'd become a car driver, admiring the view often made me miss the turn-off into Keswick.

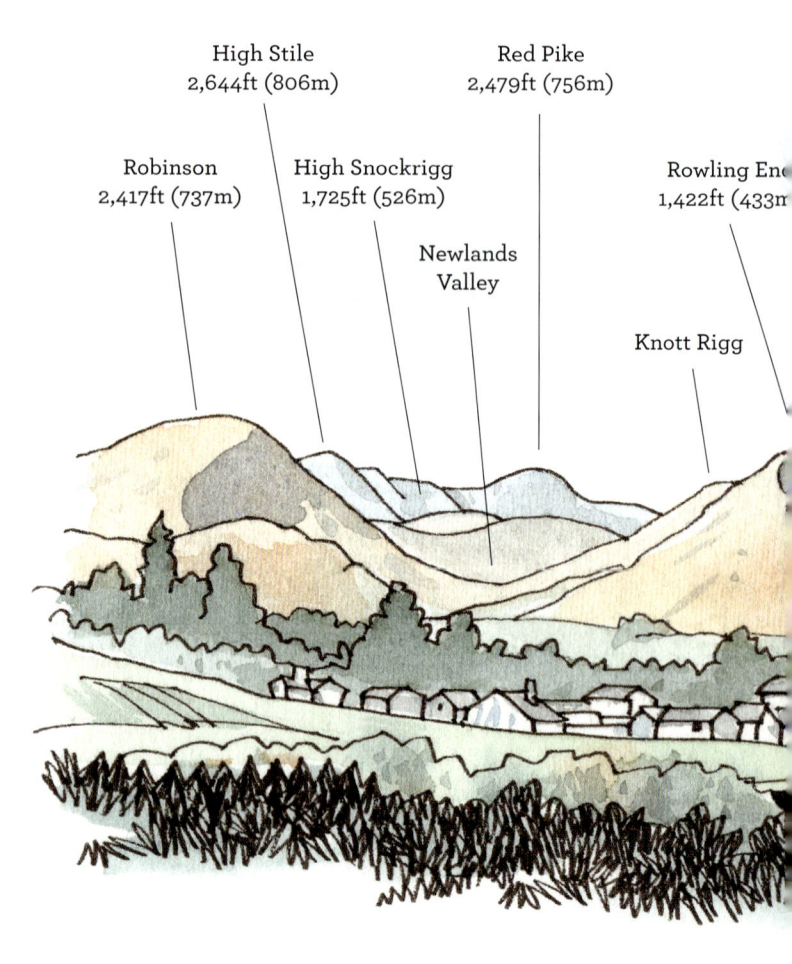

High Stile 2,644ft (806m)
Red Pike 2,479ft (756m)
Robinson 2,417ft (737m)
High Snockrigg 1,725ft (526m)
Rowling End 1,422ft (433m)
Newlands Valley
Knott Rigg

Right: Newlands fells from the old A66 road at Storms Farm.

◀ Carrying the A66 across the deep gorge of the River Greta, Greta Bridge was built of concrete during 1974–77, costing £1.5 million. The four-span structure was at the time one of the longest bridges of its type in the country. Despite furious criticism before, during and after construction, in 2000 the bridge was voted 'best concrete engineering structure of the century' by (surprise, surprise) the Concrete Society.

KESWICK

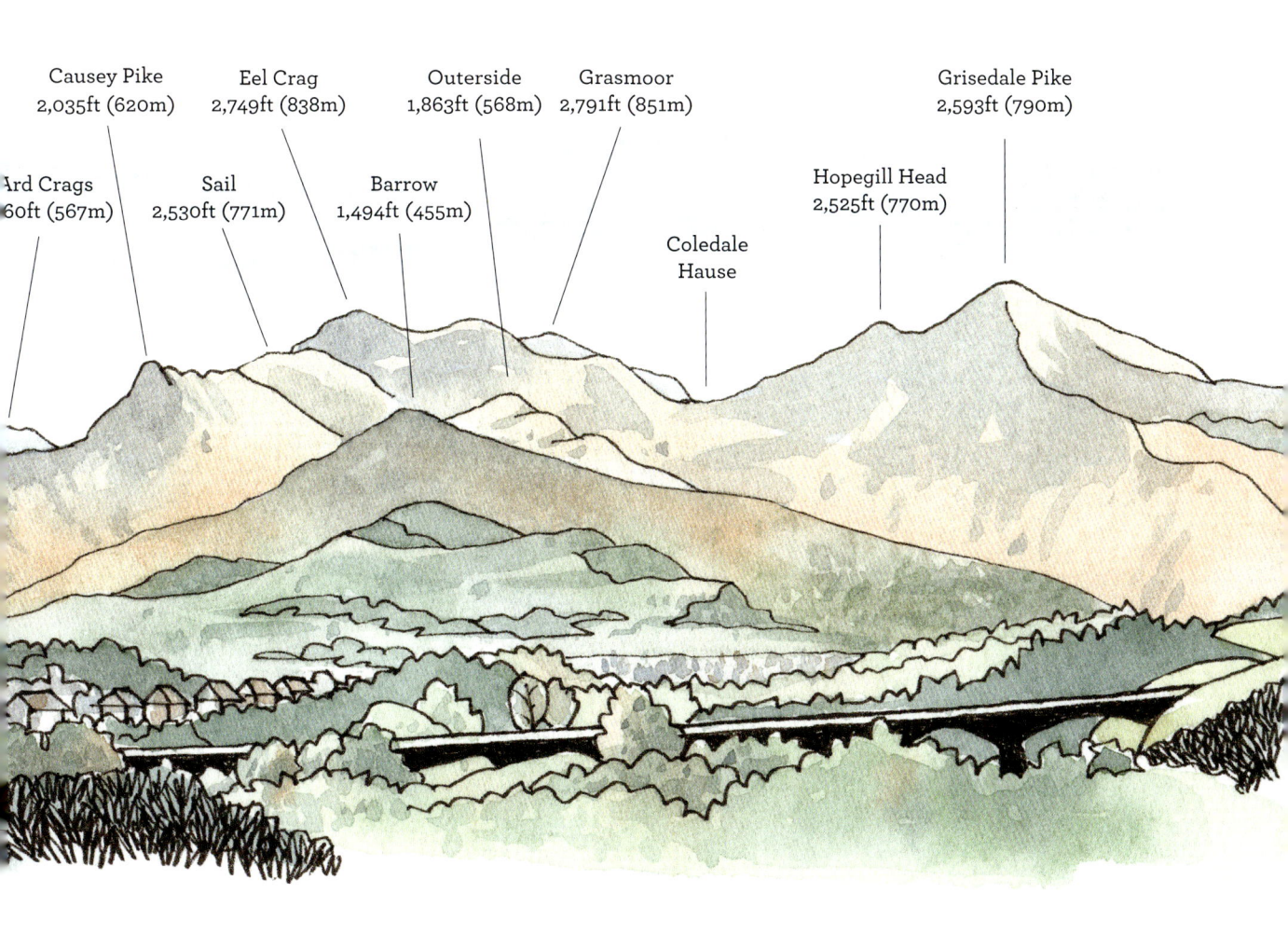

Causey Pike 2,035ft (620m)
Eel Crag 2,749ft (838m)
Outerside 1,863ft (568m)
Grasmoor 2,791ft (851m)
Grisedale Pike 2,593ft (790m)
Ard Crags ...60ft (567m)
Sail 2,530ft (771m)
Barrow 1,494ft (455m)
Hopegill Head 2,525ft (770m)
Coledale Hause

Itchy feet

By the scrag-end of the 1950s, change was underway in our remote part of the world. Coffee bars with juke boxes opened in town and electrical shops started selling gramophone records. We organised trips to Carlisle to see pop stars and marvelled at the sight and sound of electric guitars.

I bought my first 78rpm record – 'Great Balls of Fire' by Jerry Lee Lewis – to play on an old wind-up player my father had brought home. Later, he applied heat to the record and shaped it into a fashionable (at the time) plastic plant pot. Sacrilege.

> **Despite living in a rural paradise, a feeling had settled inside me that it wasn't enough.**

Everything seemed to be changing, but I wasn't. I was unhappy at home and unhappy with myself. Despite living in a rural paradise surrounded by mountains and lakes – most of which I'd never even visited yet – a feeling had settled inside me that it wasn't enough. I wanted more.

Something was telling me I should move on. I still don't know what it was – maybe my subconscious mind had decided now was the time and the restlessness I was experiencing was its way of telling me.

It was time to leave home. But how did I do it? And where was I to go?

67

KESWICK

Keswick notables

Canon Hardwicke Drummond Rawnsley (1851–1920)

Robert Southey (1774–1843)

Samuel Taylor Coleridge (1772–1834)

Sir Hugh Walpole (1884–1941)

A fierce activist for nature conservation all his life, one of Rawnsley's first campaigns helped overturn a proposal to build a railway from Buttermere to Keswick. He was a friend of the Potter family, and encouraged Beatrix to write and illustrate her first book.

But his greatest achievement was founding – with Octavia Hill and Sir Robert Hunter – the National Trust in 1893.

Another of his ideas was the Keswick School of Industrial Art, which taught creative skills to local youngsters.

An active churchman, he was vicar of Crosthwaite (1883–1917), honorary Canon of Carlisle (1893) and chaplain to King George V (1912–1920).

Hailed as 'a Titan of the Lake District' by Hunter Davies, Rawnsley is buried at Crosthwaite Church.

Despite spending most of his adult life in the Lakes, Southey wrote hardly any verse connected with the area, but he did write the original version of 'Goldilocks and the Three Bears' and an interminable children's poem about how the water comes down Lodore Falls.

A hard-working writer, he produced reams of books, novels, poems and journalism. He famously wrote the first official history of Brazil without ever visiting the country.

Southey became Poet Laureate in 1813 and, alongside Wordsworth and Coleridge, made the Lakes a centre of Romantic poetry for decades.

He died at Keswick, with the Brazilian government paying for his tomb in Crosthwaite churchyard. His memorial in the church has an epitaph written by Wordsworth.

In 1795 Coleridge met Wordsworth in Somerset and they began writing poetry together.

Coleridge had already written his most famous works, *The Rime of the Ancient Mariner* and *Kubla Khan*, when he moved his family north in 1800 to live at Greta Hall and be closer to the Wordsworths.

He became a notable walker, climbing Scafell alone – an expedition that took him nine days. He also used to visit the Wordsworths at Grasmere of an evening.

His wanderings – of foot and eye – led him to abandon his family, leaving Robert Southey to care for them at Greta Hall. By then Coleridge was addicted to opium and drink, and spent the rest of his days as an itinerant writer and lecturer. He died in Highgate, then a village north of London.

Born the Bishop of Edinburgh's son in New Zealand, Walpole was sent to school in England and never returned home. During the First World War he worked as a war correspondent for the *Daily Mail*. He was a natural storyteller and became a best-selling author in the 1920s and 30s, writing novels, short stories and screenplays. In 1924 he bought Brackenburn, a property set on the slopes of Cat Bells overlooking Derwent Water, and divided the rest of his life between there and London.

His most famous and successful books are the four *Herries Chronicle* novels, which are set in the Northern fells.

Knighted in 1937, he was buried at St John's Church, Keswick, appropriately on a terrace overlooking Derwent Water.

KESWICK

Castlerigg Stone Circle

Set on a grassy hilltop just one and a half miles east of Keswick is the finest Neolithic circle in the Lakes. Castlerigg Stone Circle consists of 39 stones arranged in an oval with a long-side diameter of 110ft. The tallest stone stands at just over seven foot, with the average height three foot. The circle is reckoned to be between 3-4,000 years old; ancient even when the Romans were here. Why the stones were erected on this spot and what their purpose was remains a mystery.

There are 17 other Neolithic circles in the Lake District, some of them more impressive, but none enjoy the marvellous setting that this one has, perched 650ft above the streets of Keswick and surrounded by some of Lakeland's finest fells.

> **My life was about to change in ways I could never have thought possible.**

Above: Castlerigg Stone Circle and Blencathra.

When I left school, the local Youth Employment Bureau found me a job as office boy at Keswick's premier architects, Hope and Davidson. I enjoyed colouring prints of working drawings and measuring up on site, but it didn't take me long to decide I didn't fancy five years of intensive study to become an architect.

One day I was called to the phone at work. It was the local Youth Employment Bureau to tell me that British Thomson-Houston (BTH) in Rugby were recruiting for engineering apprenticeships. Was I interested?

I had no idea what BTH did or where Rugby was, but I said yes immediately.

I didn't realise it at the time, but my life was about to change in ways I could never have thought possible.

Rugby

I began my apprenticeship at British Thomson-Houston in November 1960. For a shy boy from somewhere up north it was a momentous change. Rugby was the furthest I'd ever been away from the Lake District.

Together with around 300 other apprentices and students, my new home was Coton House, a country mansion converted to an all-male hostel outside town. We each shared a room with three or four others, so getting on with people was a necessity; shyness was no excuse. Residents came from all over the world and living with them was a rewarding experience.

There was always plenty to do: numerous clubs and societies, a cinema, a sports field, TV lounges and a reading room with all the daily papers. I acquired mates with uncanny abilities to win money at cards. As most of my meagre pay was spent over the weekend in Rugby pubs, I learnt how to win money and pay for the next day's lunch during the week. Lakeland seemed a long way away.

Each year we were given a free voucher for a rail trip home, which I took advantage of at Christmas. It was odd returning to Threlkeld. I'd only been away for a few weeks and already I felt like an outsider. My old pals had little to say beyond "When yer garn back?",

Above: Coton House. *Below:* Rugby School Close from a 2015 painting.

> It was odd returning to Threlkeld. I'd only been away for a few weeks and already I felt like an outsider.

and I felt sad at the gulf that had already grown between us.

In 1961 BTH had a visit from the Queen Mother. A week before she came, several apprentices were selected to practise looking as though we knew what we were doing.

On the big day I stood behind a lathe facing royal interrogation: "Where have you come from?", "What does this machine do?", "Is it difficult to operate?" The company photographers clicked away and a picture of me and the Queen mum adorned a Threlkeld council house wall for years afterwards.

Our training was a mix of theory at technical college and practice in various engineering departments, shadowing experienced workers. They were supposed to teach you the rudiments of their job, but the ones I was teamed with were more concerned with fiddling time sheets and bragging about their sexual conquests – especially if an office girl had the misfortune to walk through the factory.

Nightshift in Large Machines department was to experience a strange other-world, where workers found endless ways of filling time without doing much work. You could get a haircut, buy contraceptives, borrow a raunchy paperback or place a bet on pretty much anything. Beds were made up in the most unlikely of places. Indeed, the first job of day shift workers was to check there was no-one asleep inside their machines before turning them on.

In Test Maintenance department I shadowed an 'experienced' engineer into a high-voltage test area, enclosed in a cage of steel that theoretically you could only enter if the current was switched off. I climbed a ladder to unscrew a cover and my hair touched an overhead copper conductor. Megawatts of electricity surged through my

RUGBY

body, throwing me off the ladder. Fortunately (for me) I fell onto my colleague.

An investigation as to how we managed to enter a secure live area was ditched when it was ascertained that I was still alive – whereupon the shift supervisors' attention switched to working on their cover-up of the incident. I was sent back to Coton House to 'rest', where, energised by the unexpected bolt of electric shock treatment, I went for a long and enjoyable walk across the Warwickshire countryside.

The annual apprentice rag week was a big event in the town, with a travelling show around the villages, a procession with floats and general mischief-making. I edited a couple of rag magazines and helped build floats to my designs.

There was a flourishing music scene at Coton and in the town. The Granada Cinema showed dreadful 'B' films on a Sunday night, but the main attraction were the local bands that played during the half-hour interval. I saw the Rolling Stones at the Granada and many other big UK and American acts. A folk club in a local pub was another interest, plus a weekly trad jazz night at the town hall.

As we used to say at the time: "It was all 'app'ning."

After three years of being looked after at Coton House, we were considered sufficiently house-trained to leave and find alternative accommodation in town – usually in a furnished house or flat.

With three pals I moved into a dilapidated terraced house overlooking the hallowed close of Rugby School, where William Webb Ellis first "picked up the ball

Above: The Granada, Rugby. From a 2019 painting.
Below: An Austin A35.

and ran" to create the game of rugby.

Left to our own devices, our lifestyle could easily have drifted into full-on hedonism. With the swinging '60s in full spate and pubs, parties and dolly birds widely available, debauchery beckoned. However, we had jobs to go to and three of us went to them in suits. We had standards. So we swung when we could... at weekends.

By 1964 I'd completed most of my training and spent the last year of my apprenticeship as a draughtsman working on marine gearboxes and a nuclear power station plant.

It was interesting work and there was creative fulfilment in seeing a huge piece of machinery on the shop floor that pencil lines on my drawing board had helped create.

In my spare time I drew single-gag cartoons and had success selling some to national newspapers and magazines.

Life was good. In 1965 I even saw my hero Bob Dylan play live in Leicester during his last acoustic tour before going electric. Could life get any better?

Unexpectedly, it did. I met Maureen Hayward. Two years later we were married and I became part of a warm extended family filled with love and laughter. It was the best thing I ever did. We went on to have two wonderful children, Tim and Holly.

We began married life and a year later bought our first car, an Austin A35.

I wanted to show Maureen the Lake District, so at the first opportunity we drove north. She liked it. I heard a bugle play. Lakeland was calling me back.

RUGBY

Happy returns

In 1969 we moved to a modern terraced house in the same Rugby street we live in now. The Lakes became a regular getaway, where the landscape never failed to revive and stimulate with its mysterious magic.

Drawing straight lines at work paid the bills, but thinking up gags and drawing cartoons was far more fun. Sales were encouraging and began to feed my ambition – a quality I'd never possessed in quantity before. Previously, life just seemed to happen; I hadn't realised you could help it along a bit.

I sent some drawings to the comics department at IPC, publisher of *Buster*, *Cor!!* and *Knockout,* and received a swift reply. They were looking for artists. Was I interested? I said yes, but immediately doubted whether my drawing skills were up to it. I had to learn, fast.

The work was to draw for the comic annual books in the style of an established artist and to a written script. Enjoyment brought speed, and soon I was drawing for weekly comics. The publishers of *The Beano* and *The Dandy*, DC Thomson, got in touch and I began doing

Below left: 'Sports School' for *Shiver & Shake* annual.
Below: Syndicated cartoon.

work for them as well. Soon I was earning more in my spare time than at work; my pen was pointing the way forward.

In 1973 I took the major step of leaving full-time employment for full-time unemployment as a freelance. Maureen was pregnant with our Tim, so with hindsight it wasn't the most sensible thing to do, but it worked out OK. Holly was born a year later. Both children were born at home, and being with them from day one, sharing in their growing up, was a huge privilege.

Towards the end of the 1970s, the boom in comics faded as kids deserted pen and ink for the new technicolour attractions of computer games and animated Americana.

The comic work dried up and I had to find other ways of making money. I had no formal artistic training, but by then was confident (desperate) enough to say yes to anything I was asked to draw.

Times were tough, but in the early 1980s Survival Books came to my rescue, asking for cartoons and house illustrations for a range of how-to live books in various countries. The work has been a fruitful lifeline for me over the years – producing book covers, illustrations, cartoons and maps for numerous publications. I've even written and illustrated my own range of 'Sketchbooks' for them.

In 1986 I sent some map and house drawings to Walt Unsworth at Cicerone Press in Cumbria asking if he needed anything drawn. He didn't, but suggested that I might consider doing a book on Lakeland villages. I leaped at the chance. A door of opportunity had opened and I was able to re-forge my relationship with the Lake District.

For research I visited villages I'd never been to before, saw scenes I'd never seen before and drew familiar places too, adding a further dimension to their appeal. I honed my skills producing scores of line drawings. *Lakeland Villages* went on to receive an award at the 1989 Lakeland Book of the Year.

RUGBY

Lakeland Towns followed in 1992 and *Lakeland Panoramas* in 1995. My affection for Lakeland was further enhanced by walking the Cumbria Way from Ulverston to Carlisle and producing a guide to both it and the Allerdale Ramble.

As our children grew, we kept visiting the Lakes, going on walks and watching our kids playing in becks just as I'd done years before. Friends and family also came, and I escorted them around Lakeland as proud as a billionaire showing off his Mayfair mansion.

Back in Rugby I pulled on my walking boots and self-published a couple of books on local country walks. They've sold well over the years, but especially recently as walking has become ever-more popular.

I draw strips for *Lakeland Walker* and *Cumbria Magazine*, which keeps me in touch and allows me to comment on local issues.

Family members still live in the north Lakes and we'll keep visiting as long as we're able. These days we're content to eat our sandwiches on Honister Pass summit or enjoy carrot cake and coffee at Caldbeck. There are always new places to explore and memories to relive of familiar ones – just soaking up the scenery, happy to enjoy it together.

Some philosophers maintain that random happenings in life prepare us for something bigger, even though we don't realise it at the time. My leaving Lakeland was always a preparation for coming back.

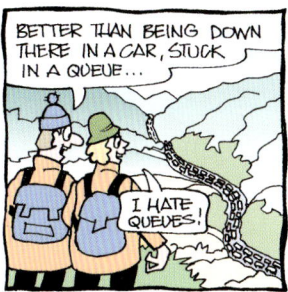

Above: Fellsiders for *Lakeland Walker*.
Right: House for Survival Books.
Far right: Friends for Philip Allan Publishers.
Bottom right: Self-published walks book.
Below: The Lakers for *Cumbria Magazine*.

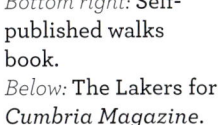

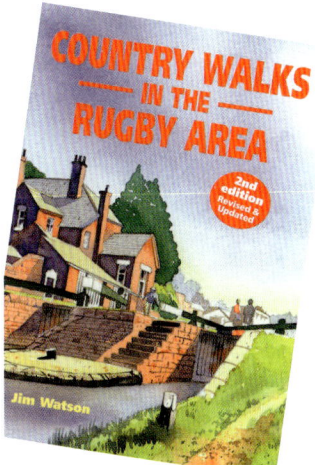

Derwent Water

The Romantic ideal

Widest of all the lakes, Derwent Water is around three miles long and just over a mile wide, with a maximum depth of 72ft. The lake has four main islands plus nine smaller ones.

The western and eastern sides are deeply wooded, with Cat Bells and Walla Crag framing the scene. The Skiddaw massif dominates the north, formed from some of the oldest rock in Europe, draped in heather and arranged in a series of variable-sized cones like furry playthings.

But though easy to climb, this is no toy

Below: Borrowdale from Friar's Crag.

mountain. Skiddaw stands only around 150ft short of Scafell Pike and is notoriously cold across the top, even in summer. The old boy deserves to be treated with respect.

Borrowdale stretches invitingly to the south. This is the Lake District in miniature. Nowhere else in the Lakes are the three components of the Romantic ideal – rocks, trees and water – so perfectly arranged as they are here. With Derwent Water and Borrowdale on your doorstep you need never go anywhere else. And for years I never did.

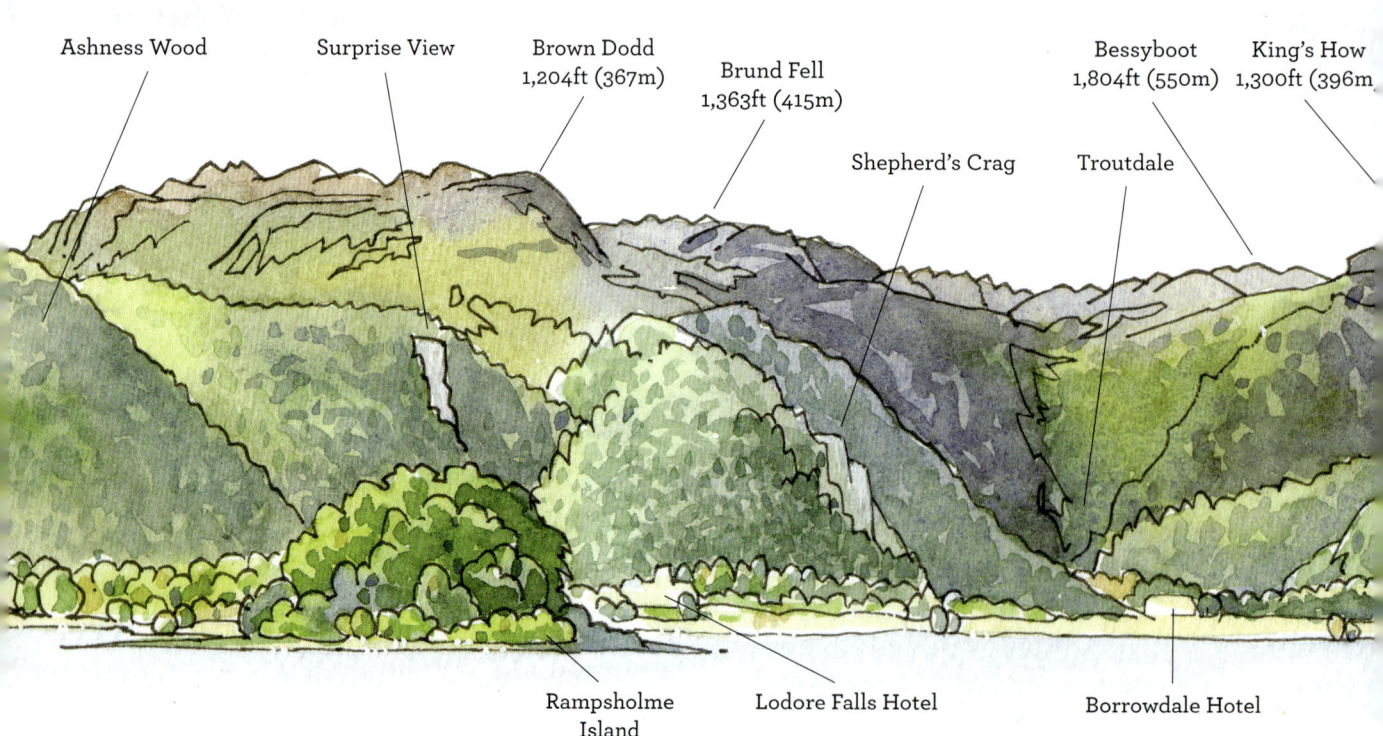

Ashness Wood · Surprise View · Brown Dodd 1,204ft (367m) · Brund Fell 1,363ft (415m) · Shepherd's Crag · Bessyboot 1,804ft (550m) · Troutdale · King's How 1,300ft (396m)

Rampsholme Island · Lodore Falls Hotel · Borrowdale Hotel

DERWENT WATER

▼ Friar's Crag is one of the most visited viewpoints in Lakeland. It's a low headland of rock topped by scraggy Scots pines and hardly deserves the 'crag' tag. However, as a vantage point, it is beyond compare. The art critic and social thinker John Ruskin, who has a memorial on the crag, rated the view of Borrowdale from Friar's Crag among his top three in Europe – though he was prone to hyperbole. According to him Keswick was "too beautiful to live in".

Derwent Island became a sanctuary for German miners in 1565 when they were badly received by locals. In the 18th century the eccentric Joseph Pocklington built a house and various follies on the island. The Marshall family then lived there for over a century, before handing ownership to the National Trust in 1951.

Rampsholme Island once had a bloomery for smelting iron ore, while St Herbert's Island is named after the seventh-century hermit immortalised by Wordsworth.

The lake that has everything, Derwent Water even has a 'ghost' island, periodically rising from the lake bed on a cushion of marsh gas near Lodore.

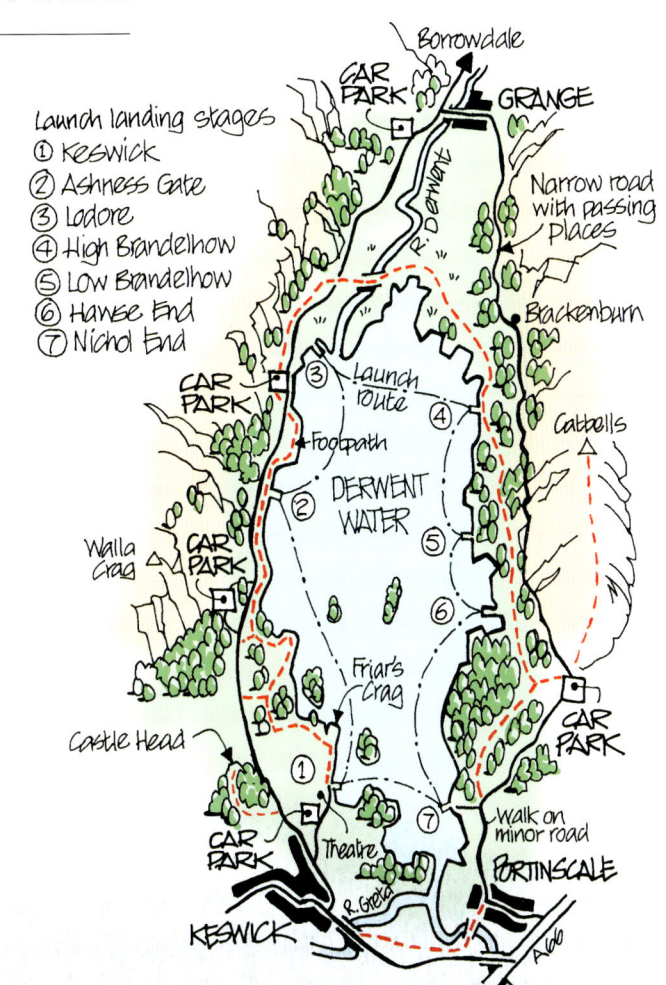

Launch landing stages
① Keswick
② Ashness Gate
③ Lodore
④ High Brandelhow
⑤ Low Brandelhow
⑥ Hawse End
⑦ Nichol End

Glaramara 2,560ft (780m)
Esk Hause
Castle Crag 985ft (300m)
Great End 2,984ft (910m)
Scafell Pike 3,210ft (978m)
Nitting Haws
Manesty Park

DERWENT WATER

You can walk all the way around Derwent Water, with only a short stretch away from the shoreline. Equally popular are trips on one of the popular launches that have run a regular service around the lake since 1904. Two are over 100 years old – still in service and built of Burma teak, originally for the use of Lodore Hotel visitors.

The boat landings are usually busy with flocks of tourists and Canada geese. The view across Derwent Island is terrific, but I prefer the one from nearby Crow Park, where the foreground is taken up by picnickers and landscape photographers.

Below: **The boat landings at Keswick.**

Accessed from Crow Park, Isthmus Bay used to be a popular place to swim in the lake during the 1950s. One of our games teachers decided that for gym we should run down to the bathing landing, swim for half an hour then run back to school for our French lesson. Fortunately, it was during the summer, so the lake wasn't frozen, but the freshness of the water was still… energising.

Those swimming trips didn't last for long; our fastidious French teacher soon complained about her lessons being adulterated by males in the class sweating profusely and steaming-up the windows.

Maiden Moor

Cat Bells
1,481ft (451m)

Derwent Island

Robinson
2,417ft (737m)

High Stile
2,644ft (806m)

Rowling End
1,422ft (433m)

Newlands

DERWENT WATER

Another games teacher had the bright idea of transporting us on the back of a lorry to Manesty, from where we had to run back to school. My pal Chas – ever on the ball and who knew everyone who mattered in Keswick – led me to the High Brandelhow landing and hailed a passing launch. We then enjoyed a leisurely trip down the lake with a boatload of Japanese tourists taking our photos. A trot across Crow Park brought us back to school to be greeted with surprise (and not a little suspicion) by the teacher.

Above: **A Derwent Water launch.**

▼ Friar's Crag is thought to be named after the friars who embarked from here to visit St Herbert, who brought Christianity to the Lakes in the seventh century and lived on Derwent Water's biggest island – now called St Herbert's Island.

Beatrix Potter, who spent family holidays at Lingholm across the lake, was a fan of the island and christened it Owl Island in *The Tale of Squirrel Nutkin*. Friar's Crag appears in Arthur Ransome's *Swallows and Amazons* as the children's lookout spot, Darien.

Causey Pike
2,035ft (620m)

Eel Crag
2,749ft (838m)

ndelhow Park

DERWENT WATER

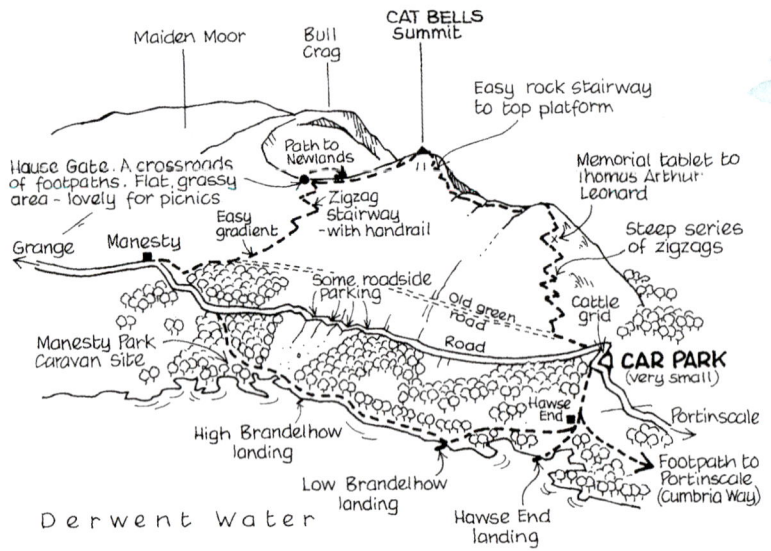

▲ Seen from across the lake Cat Bells looks cuddly and inviting – an easy-peasy walk for a picnic with the family. And indeed it is; we've done it a number of times.

However, from the north end, the ascent begins with a steep and sweaty climb, leading to a broad ridge from where you can admire the exceptional views. Another short scramble takes you onto the rocky summit. The genuinely easy-peasy route – it has steps and a handrail – is from Manesty.

The views north to Skiddaw and west into Newlands are sensational. When Ruskin maintained that the most aesthetic views are from lowly fells, he must have been thinking of Cat Bells.

Above: **Manesty Park.**

Below: **The view from Cat Bells' summit.**

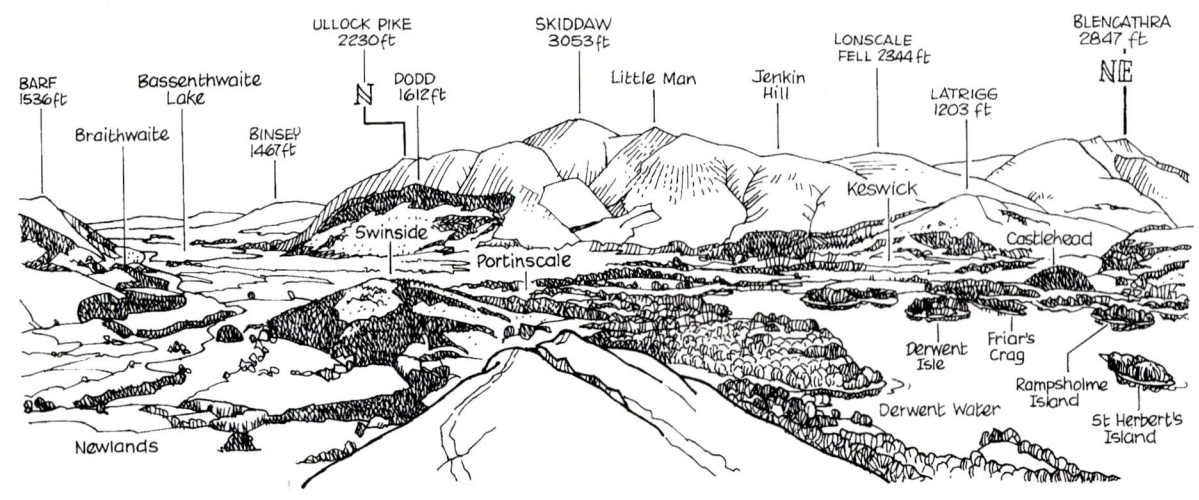

DERWENT WATER

The oak woods along the western shore of Derwent Water are one of the lake's many glories. When they were put up for sale in 1902, Canon Rawnsley launched a public appeal to raise £6,500 to buy them.

His appeal reached its target within five months and Brandelhow Woods became the National Trust's first acquisition in Lakeland.

Below: Brandelhow Point and, *lower left,* part of Brandelhow woods.

Call me biased, but I find it difficult to find any fault with Derwent Water. From any vantage point it looks lovely. There's a peaceful beauty about it – 'nobbet chocolate box beauty', cynics might say. True, but I have no problem with chocolate boxes… At Derwent Water it's there already – in every weather and mood: constant perfection.

Ashness

I first saw Ashness's packhorse bridge when I was about 13 and on a field trip with the Scouts. The view was great, but I didn't realise at the time that Ashness Bridge was world famous. I was more interested in the elderly gent with grey, windswept hair, tweed baggy trousers and a pleasant smile who manned a five-barred gate across the road where it emerged from the wood onto the fellside.

He was Vivian Fisher and his role was to open the gate for vehicles on their way to Watendlath. Passengers thanked him and dropped money into his cloth flat cap. Walkers stopped to chat while he fed breadcrumbs to the chaffinches. Bathed in Lakeland sunshine, it looked to me an excellent career choice. Where did I apply!?

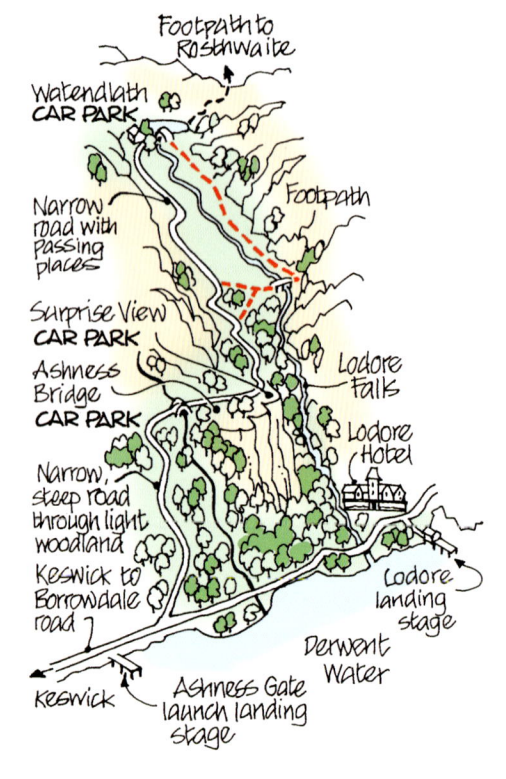

Our Scout troop was meant to be building a rope bridge across Barrow Beck near the stone hut in the gill. It seemed a bit pointless to me as there was already a perfectly serviceable stone bridge over the beck.

As boredom set in, I sneaked off to explore the magnificent woods that cloak the hillsides. Oak is the dominant species here, with these 'Atlantic oak woods' an example of temperate rainforest. The area is designated as a Special Area of Conservation (SAC).

The woods are home to a wide range of bird species and large mammals, including red and roe deer. Red squirrels are fairly common thanks to a programme of grey squirrel control.

Left: **Ashness Bridge from the south.**

ASHNESS

I've drawn Ashness Bridge a number of times. For a different view I like to climb down below the bridge so it becomes centre of interest in the composition.

After heavy rain, water fizzes under the arch, searching for new routes downhill through glistening rocks worn smooth by decades of water passage. Plants and mosses thrive among the steaming, soggy action.

On these artistic field trips I often return with a classic 'Threlkeld soaker' in one of my inadequate cheap trainers, but with a sketchbook dripping with authentic energy and atmosphere.

Above: **Ashness Bridge from the north.**
Below: **A launch leaving Lodore landing, seen from Surprise View.**

I stumbled on nearby Surprise View by chance. One minute I was picking my way through tree roots. The next I was tottering on the edge of a drop high above the lake. I was alone, in Scout uniform, and I felt like a latter-day David Livingstone discovering the Victoria Falls. Could I keep this awesome place secret for only me to enjoy?

No chance. These days Surprise View has a broad, well-trodden platform, with a car park nearby ensuring you are unlikely to be alone.

However, the airy scene remains undiminished. I go back whenever I can and I'm always surprised at how surprising it is.

WATENDLATH

◀ Watendlath is a classic example of a Lake District hanging valley. As melting glacial ice fashioned the large valleys, it also left little sub-troughs at higher levels. Watendlath Beck drops nearly 600ft before joining Derwent Water. The final descent is spectacular (after heavy rain) over Lodore Falls.

Watendlath's tarn, packhorse bridge and huddle of farm buildings have been photographed, filmed and painted in all manner of colourful compositions. Beautifully situated in a basin of gentle fells, it has a charm that is difficult to resist. The narrow road from Ashness ends at the hamlet, but by far the best way to get to Watendlath is to walk along the bank of Watendlath Beck from above Ashness Bridge. Another, shorter route is on the old packhorse road from Rosthwaite.

Furness Abbey records mention Watendlath as part of the Abbey's estate in 1209. An ancient field system can still be seen at the south end of the tarn, and the first settlers were 10th-century Norsemen, who named the valley 'Vatns Endi', meaning 'end of the lake'.

The tiny hamlet is a disorganised collection of slate-built farms, barns and outbuildings, some rendered and painted white. Dry-stone walls and gnarled old trees add to the rural charm.

Left: The packhorse bridge over Watendlath Beck.

WATENDLATH

Years ago when I was wearing my 'Proudly showing off Lakeland to Rugby pals' hat, I led my family of Maureen and our two children, plus the Cooper family with their three youngsters, on the route from Rosthwaite to Watendlath.

Everyone seemed to enjoy it – and no child fell in the water despite their best efforts.

When asked later what they'd enjoyed most about their day out in glorious countryside the children said: "Feeding the birds in the tea garden – and seeing the runner, Brendan Foster, in the car park."

Kids, eh?

Left: Watendlath Tarn.

Left: A stone hut that I like to think of as a 'Man Cave'.
Right: Barn doors – slightly out of line.

▶ Judith Paris is a fictional character in the famous *Herries Chronicle* books written by Hugh Walpole (*see page 66*). Judith lived at Watendlath with her husband, who used the valley as a hideout from his smuggling activities at Whitehaven.

In 1937, Walpole was asked to settle a dispute between two Watendlath residents who both claimed to live in the 'Judith Paris house'.

Walpole, a diplomat of the old school, declared that he'd not based his heroine's house on any one building in the hamlet. Despite this, a farmhouse still carries a slate sign announcing it as 'The Home of Judith Paris'.

GRANGE

Grange

Furness Abbey owned most of Borrowdale in the 14th century and a 'grange' was established to administer local affairs. None of that original settlement remains, but some of the houses in Grange are reputed to have monastic stone in their walls.

The tiny hamlet is beautifully situated where the River Derwent widens to around 85 yards and splits, so the graceful stone bridge, built in 1675, requires two arches. After periods of heavy rain, epic amounts of water flow through here.

Centuries of erosion have resulted in heaps of beautifully smooth stones spread across the river sides. The water is remarkably clear, enhancing the colours of the stones in the riverbed to perfection.

Attractive and genteel, modern Grange marks its ecclesiastical past by having both a Methodist Chapel by the bridge and a church, Holy Trinity, built in 1860 with churchyard walls of slate slabs set on end.

A significant geological change can be seen in the fells on the west side of the valley. The craggy fells to the south are hard Borrowdale Volcanic slate, which splits well for roofing purposes. The more smooth-sided Maiden Moor, spreading north to Cat Bells, is formed of softer Skiddaw slate.

It's one of the oldest rocks in Europe, but it easily shatters into small pieces and is useless for building.

Above: Grange Bridge and the River Derwent.
Below: Holy Trinity Church.

GRANGE

Above: Central Grange. The farm on the right was the model for the house of Rogue Herries in the quartet of Lakeland novels by Hugh Walpole, who lived a mile away.
Below: The Bowder Stone.

The Bowder Stone

Hidden in the woods near Grange, the Bowder Stone is an immense rock, some 30ft high by 60ft long and weighing around 2,000 tons. It rests on a narrow crest, like the keel of a ship, and looks likely to roll over at any moment, despite standing firm since being dumped here by an Ice Age glacier.

The stone was established as a tourist attraction by the wealthy and eccentric Joseph Pocklington in 1798. He constructed a ladder so tourists could stand on its summit. Another of his additions was a cottage by the rock as a home for an old woman to – as the marketeer said – "lend the place quaint atmosphere".

In 2019 the National Trust installed the latest of many ladders to the top. This one is of metal, and, unlike Pocklington's, it conforms to all modern safety standards.

Rosthwaite

Set on a rocky knoll between two lively rivers, Rosthwaite stands at the centre of Borrowdale's flat valley floor. Craggy and colourful fells, their lower slopes swathed in trees, surround the settlement.

There's more to Rosthwaite than first meets the eye. The main road squeezes through a bottleneck and negotiates an awkward bend past the Scafell Hotel before continuing up the valley. The village itself lies away from this road – a place of countless nooks and crannies, whitewashed cottages and comfy lodging places. There's also a car park and an excellent tearoom at Yew Tree Farm along a side road by the village hall.

A popular walk starts from here to Castle Crag, the 'rotten tooth' prominent in the Jaws of Borrowdale and once the site of an Iron Age fort. The sensational all-round views from the summit are rich reward for the short if steep and rocky climb, partly through the ancient detritus of an abandoned slate quarry.

A return to Rosthwaite along the riverside makes a perfect introduction to one of my favourite parts of the Lakes. Wainwright labelled it "the loveliest square mile in Lakeland," and I wouldn't argue with him.

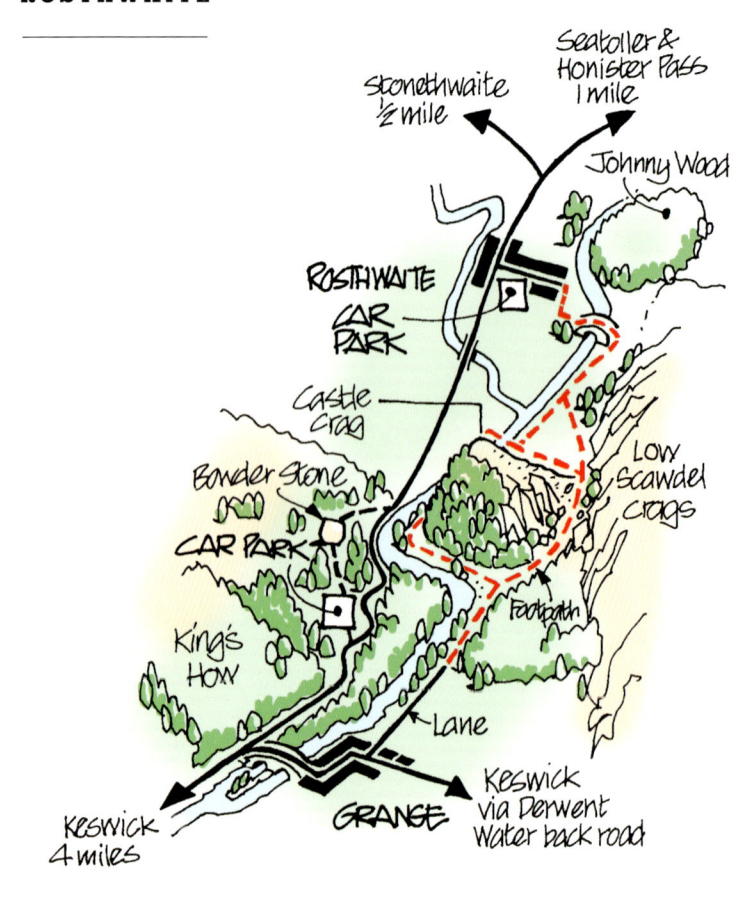

Below left: **Yew Tree Farm.**
Right: **The Rosthwaite bottleneck.**

ROSTHWAITE

Above: **Castle Crag.**
Below: **The view north from Castle Crag.**

Ullock Pike
1,730ft (680m)

Carl Side
2,420ft (738m)

Skiddaw
3,053ft (931m)

Latrigg
1,203ft (367m)

Lonscale Fell
2,344ft (714m)

Walla Crag
1,234ft (376m)

Dodd
1,612ft (491m)

Blencathra
2,847ft (868m)

Jenkin Hill

Keswick

Derwent Water

slopes of Catbells

Grange

King's How

STONETHWAITE

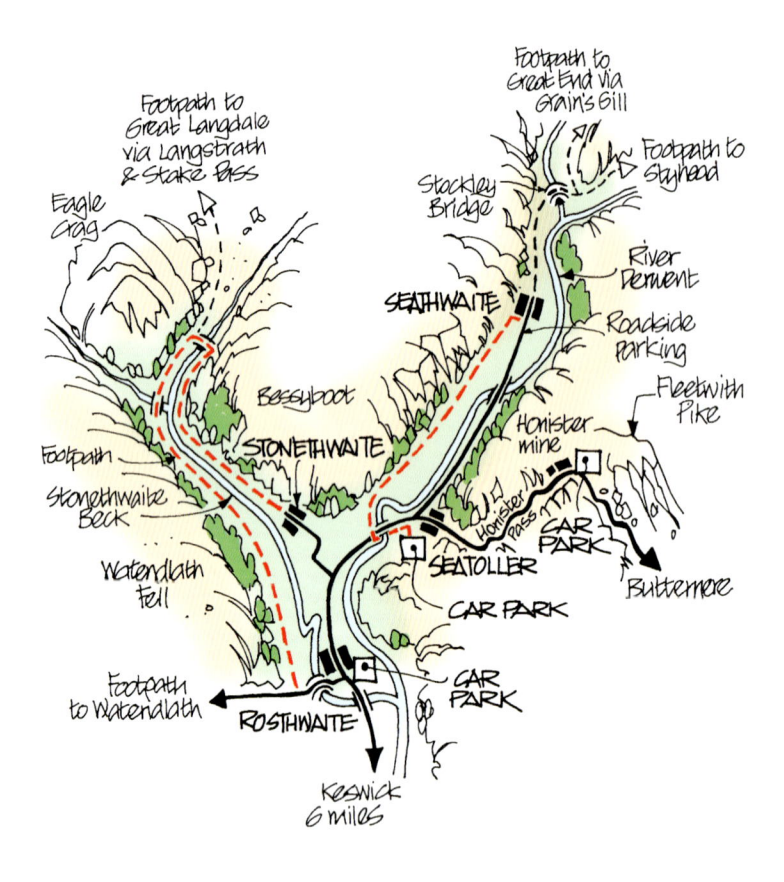

Stonethwaite

Beyond Rosthwaite, Borrowdale splits, the left side-valley heading to Stonethwaite, the right to Seatoller and Seathwaite.

Stonethwaite is only a couple of miles long, but has all the attributes of classic Lakeland: wooded slopes, fearsome crags, a lively beck and one of the prettiest hamlets in the district. The narrow road ends at a campsite and the rest of the valley is left to walkers. Some climb up Langstrath and cross Stake Pass into Great Langdale. Others take Greenup Gill to the left of Eagle Crag bound for Grasmere.

When researching my *Guide to the Cumbria Way* in 1996, I crossed Stake Pass from Great Langdale to Borrowdale. The descent down Langstrath – barren, narrow and rock-strewn – was stark. But turning into the lush Stonethwaite valley was like entering a promised land.

> **❝** I've drawn this building in Stonethwaite a number of times and every time I see the real thing I want to draw it again.

In medieval times most of Borrowdale belonged to the mighty Furness Abbey, but Watendlath, Langstrath and Seathwaite were all owned by the equally important Fountains Abbey in Yorkshire. With two huge landowners rubbing shoulders, there must have been lively disputes.

Eagle Crag dominates the head of Stonethwaite, a great bastion and focal point of the valley. Golden Eagles were documented here in 1777, but the chance of seeing one these days is nil.

▲ Yew Tree Farmhouse, Stonethwaite. A Grade II listed building, dated late 17th century. I've drawn this building in Stonethwaite a number of times and every time I see the real thing I want to draw it again. It has all the attributes I like: white walls, colourful garden, lovely tree, dry-stone walls and bits-and-bobs lying about. One day I hope to do a version I'm happy with!

SEATOLLER

Seatoller

The Borrowdale valley road divides again at the hamlet of Seatoller. The main highway climbs over Honister Pass to Buttermere, while a narrow road strikes off left to Seathwaite and the big mountains.

Seatoller is pleasant enough, but nobody stays here for long; motorists or walkers are all on their way somewhere else.

In the 16th century the hillsides here were home to a hugely profitable plumbago (or graphite) mining industry. Apart from being used in pencils (hence the famous Keswick pencil industry), plumbago has other applications – including in the production of cannonballs. At one time the mineral was so valuable it could only be transported under armed guard. The yield gradually diminished and the last Seathwaite mine closed in 1836.

Above left: **Seatoller.**
Below: **The road to Seathwaite.**

Grains Gill

Great End
2,990ft (910m)

Seathwaite Fell
2,073ft (632m)

Styhead Gill

Base Brown
2,119ft (646m)

SEATHWAITE

Slopes of Glaramara
Grains Gill
Great End 2,984ft (910m)
Slopes of Seathwaite Fell

Seathwaite

The most southerly point of the long Borrowdale valley and a settlement of only a few farm buildings, Seathwaite is nationally famous as the wettest inhabited place in England – although that record has been recently challenged. Around 3,500mm of rain falls on Seathwaite in an average year, while in September 1966 127mm of rain fell in a single hour. The resulting flood swept away nearby Stockley Bridge, which was rebuilt in its original packhorse bridge style.

Records were shattered in November 2009 when the hamlet received 314.4mm of rain in 24 hours. It was the highest rainfall measured in a single day since meteorological records began in 1727.

Without question Seathwaite can be wet. It's also well loved by fell walkers – to whom wet weather is a way of life – as the gateway to paradise; the great fells of Lakeland. Popular routes to Scafell Pike, Great Gable and Glaramara all begin and end here.

Above: **Stockley Bridge.**
Below: **Seathwaite.**

Newlands

For around five glorious miles, Newlands valley stretches south from Braithwaite to the great cliffs of Dale Head. Newlands Hause is the high point of a narrow but often busy route over to Buttermere. The rest of the valley is a sanctuary of meadows, scattered farms and a winding river with packhorse bridges. Time moves unhurriedly here.

My first visit to Newlands was on serious business: a hike to gain my Scouts First Class badge. This was the final challenge before reaching the upper echelons of Scout hierarchy.

Our mission was to complete a journey of at least 15 miles, camp overnight, cook two meals and compile a log.

With blue sky and sunshine overhead, I strode out in full walking gear including haversack, sleeping bag and, for the first time, walking boots – wellies were considered too common for the Scouts.

My gear was all borrowed, most of it from Alan, my companion on the walk. He came from a farming family and was much more capable of roughing it than me. In fact, Alan was everything that I wasn't – organised, efficient and keen to get the job done. I tended to linger, looking at the scenery and making sketches in my notebook.

Living at Threlkeld, I thought I was used to Lakeland beauty but Newlands was, and still is, a magical eye-opener – difficult to define, but easy to love.

Our route followed the old miners' track across the foot of Cat Bells. We picked our way through mine workings and climbed into the dark shadows of Dale Head and High Spy. Eventually we clambered onto Rigg Head near Dale Head Tarn. I was elated with the exciting ascent and, as we searched for the path down into Borrowdale, I started to feel a bit like a proper hiker. Which bit, I'm not sure.

We made camp at Rosthwaite and cooked the statutory two meals – evening and breakfast. This involved sausages, beans, eggs and bacon, soon sizzling thanks to Alan's campfire culinary skills. My involvement was restricted to eating only.

Sleeping outside on grass inevitably brought on my asthma, but after packing up in the morning we wandered down to Derwent Water and took a launch back to Keswick and a bus home.

Being house-bound with my chest for a few days enabled me to complete the log of our journey, including illustrations of places and things we'd seen. We both gained our First Class badges and my log received a special mention. Maybe when I grow up, I remember thinking, I could be a rural sketcher!

When I was at Keswick School I sat behind a girl who lived in Newlands. She had wonderful Pre-Raphaelite hair, an easy smile and a gentle but confident demeanour; concentration in class wasn't easy. At the time I had no idea where Newlands was, but if she lived there, I thought, it must be a mystical and romantic place. My teenage fantasy turned out not to be far wrong... about the valley that is. Though by the time I finally visited, my ethereal girl – and her celestial castle – had drifted quietly away... like many of life's idle dreams.

Left: **Newlands Church.** A handy place to pop in and give thanks for the valley's many blessings.

NEWLANDS

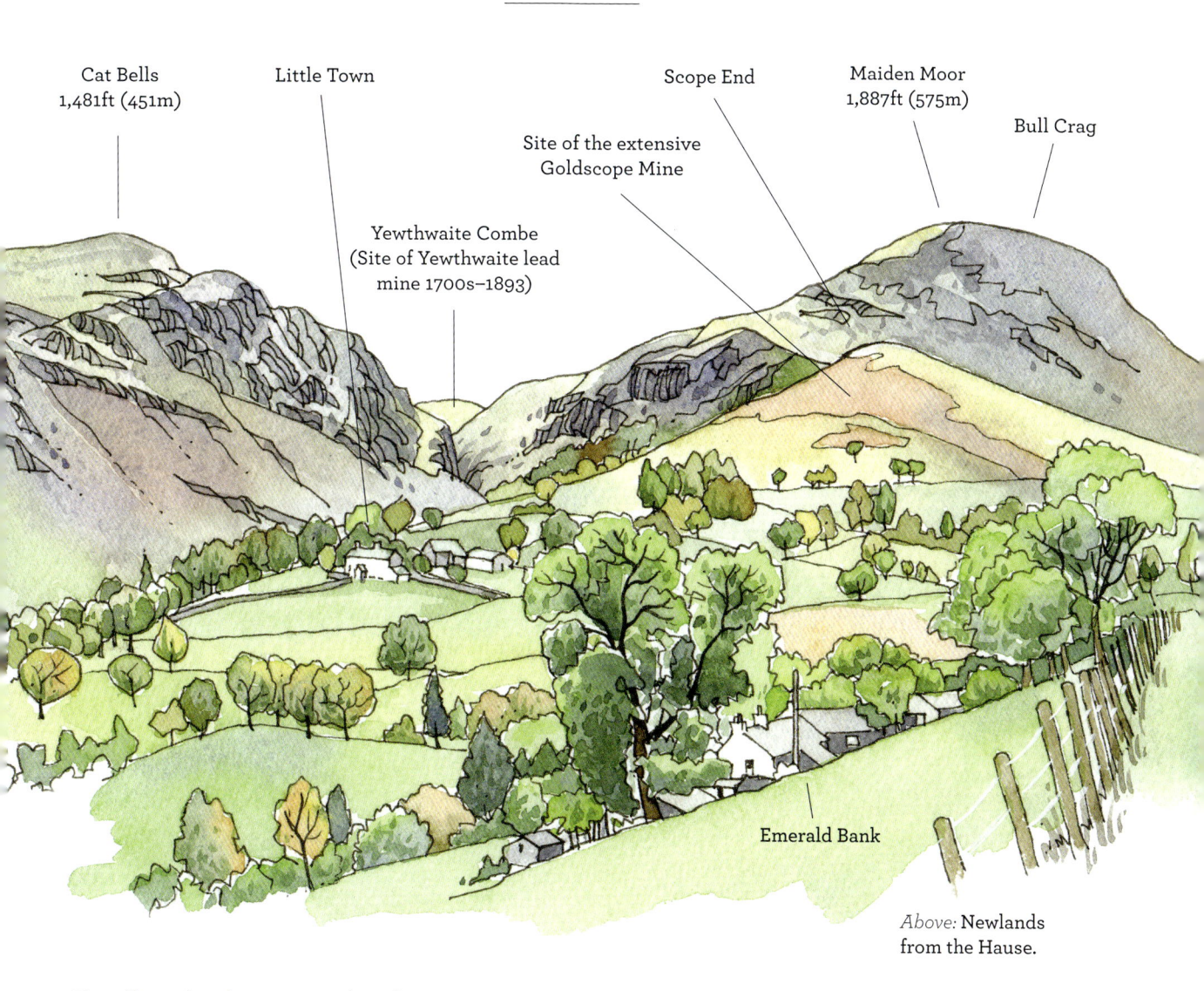

Cat Bells
1,481ft (451m)

Little Town

Scope End

Maiden Moor
1,887ft (575m)

Bull Crag

Site of the extensive
Goldscope Mine

Yewthwaite Combe
(Site of Yewthwaite lead
mine 1700s–1893)

Emerald Bank

Above: Newlands from the Hause.

▶ The village of Little Town must have been named by someone having a laugh. The tiny settlement is no more than a farm and a few cottages, even if it was inspirational enough for Beatrix Potter to include it in *The Tale of Mrs. Tiggy-Winkle*.

Maybe the medieval miners named it. Miners traditionally have a dry sense of humour, though working in the Newlands mines can never have been a barrel of laughs. The most famous, Goldscope, was worked day and night for six centuries, with lead, copper, silver and gold yielded. Extraction became ever more difficult and the mine closed around 1920.

Cockermouth

Beer, water and Wordsworth's woes

For some reason the National Park boundary excludes Cockermouth, undertaking a ruthless loop to keep it out. It's a pity, as this friendly old town deserves to be included. I have a soft spot for Cockermouth, fostered while researching my *Lakeland Towns* book.

The Romans were first to make a lasting impression here. In the second century AD they built a fort, Derventio, at the junction of three important roads linking Maryport, Penrith and Carlisle, near what is now the village of Papcastle.

Another settlement gradually developed a mile away at the junction of the Derwent and Cocker rivers. Already strategically superior, this became the centre of power when a timber castle was built around 1140. Stone from the ruins of the Roman fort was used to rebuild the castle in 1220.

King Henry III was so impressed with this settlement that he awarded Cockermouth a market charter – only the second in Cumberland. The town rapidly grew in importance, and by the 17th century it was the county's main trading centre.

Medieval Cockermouth stretched between the two hills occupied by the castle and All Saints Church. At the start of the 19th century the town had over 40 industrial sites, many of them water-powered mills along the Derwent and Cocker Rivers. Corn, wood and cotton were mainstays, with tanning and hat-making also significant trades.

COCKERMOUTH

Since then, industry has all but died, and people have had to travel elsewhere for employment. Many used to work at the Sellafield nuclear plant on the West Cumbria coast and – rumour has it – a good number of feet in the town were kept warm in winter by BNFL protective socks.

Cockermouth Castle is a sizeable but part-ruined Norman stronghold owned over the years by a series of powerful northern families. Deep inside the walls there are a couple of oubliette dungeons. Prisoners were lowered into these windowless pits through a hole in the ceiling. Escape was impossible.

Ever since the castle was built there's been a brewery on site, using water from a well under the sandstone walls. At the end of the 19th century the family firm of Jennings took over the premises after honing its brewing skills in nearby Lorton. Though modernised, the plant still uses traditional brewing methods to keep Cumbrian pubs topped up.

Below: Market Place in the centre of town.

COCKERMOUTH

◀ Sadly the Mayo Monument in the centre of Cockermouth's main street doesn't commemorate the dressing you put on sandwiches – which is far better known than the statesman the white marble statue *actually* honours.

Richard Southwell Bourke, sixth Earl of Mayo, was MP for Cockermouth before being appointed Viceroy to India in 1869. He achieved fame in 1872 when visiting a penal colony in the Andaman Islands where he was – as the local paper indelicately reported it – "Stabbed in the Andamans" by a convict. He subsequently died.

His monument was erected in 1875 and survived its own unprovoked attack in 1964, when it was hit by a petrol tanker. The statue toppled over but remained intact; the tanker was a write-off.

Cockermouth's broad and straight Main Street developed in the 19th century around the town's market area, where hiring fairs were held. Pollarded lime trees line the attractive street, which boasts a large proportion of independent shops including a traditional butcher, baker, fishmonger and greengrocer. There are also numerous pubs, restaurants, cafés, antique and gift shops, plus an excellent bookshop.

The 16th-century Trout Inn at the western end of Main Street was a favourite of crooner and Hollywood legend Bing Crosby, who liked to fish for salmon in the Derwent.

The town has a history of devastating floods – unsurprising considering the amount of water that has to pass through the town before reaching the sea at Workington.

The wide catchment of the Derwent and Cocker includes Blencathra, Borrowdale, Derwent Water, Skiddaw, Bassenthwaite, Buttermere, Crummock Water, Loweswater and, to some extent, Thirlmere.

In November 2009 over 200 people had to be rescued by helicopter or boat when the water level in the town centre rose to 2.5 metres (8ft 2in), flowing at a rate of 25 knots along Main Street. Many historic buildings were damaged, as were a number of bridges. Recovery was slow, but the town was back on its feet by the summer of 2011.

Cockermouth was particularly affected in 2015 when Storm Desmond brought 36 hours of intense rainfall and the town was inundated for the fourth time since 2005. Storm defences were overwhelmed and 500 properties were flooded.

Left: Tony Harrison's butchers shop and the United Reformed Church in Main Street.
Right: Wordsworth House.

COCKERMOUTH

▶ Cockermouth's most famous building is Wordsworth House, a fine Georgian building where William Wordsworth was born in 1770, the second eldest in a family of five. His father, John, was a solicitor who worked for wealthy landowner Sir James Lowther; the house went with the job.

The children's mother, Anne, died when William was eight, so, with his sister Dorothy, he was packed off to live with relations in Penrith. He spent an unhappy year there before being sent to school at Hawkshead. In 1783 their father died after catching a chill in a Buttermere downpour, and the Wordsworth family link with Cockermouth was broken.

The National Trust administer the house as a Wordsworth memorial. A bust of the poet was unveiled in a garden opposite the house in 1970, the bicentenary of his birth.

COCKERMOUTH

The 150ft-tall spire of All Soul's Church towers over the town, forming a landmark for miles around. Impressively Early English in style, the church replaced an earlier one that burnt down in 1850.

The largest east window (*pictured left*) commemorates William Wordsworth. His father, who died aged 42 in 1783, is buried in a corner of the churchyard.

The church stands on Kirkgate amongst a wonderful collection of unspoilt classical late 17th and 18th-century terraced housing, cobbled paving and curving lanes, which run steeply down to the River Cocker. Most buildings are of traditional slate and stone construction with thick walls and green Skiddaw slate roofs.

Significantly, most of the cottages have been rendered and painted in a variety of bright colours – an inspired feature of this central part of town. The effect is both startling and rather uplifting.

Left: **All Soul's Church.**
Below: **The panorama across the River Derwent to Main Street and Crown Street.**

Wordsworth House

Christ Church

Trout Hotel

COCKERMOUTH

Cockermouth's rich industry was mainly based on the north side of the River Derwent. The mills and factories are mostly long gone now, but small modern businesses are bringing new life to some of the old buildings.

Cockermouth cricket ground is nearby, where a young Ben Stokes learned his craft before going on to play for Durham and finding world stardom in the England team.

Fletcher Christian, leader of the HMS Bounty mutiny, was born in the village of Eaglesfield near Cockermouth. John Dalton, the father of modern atomic theory, was born in the same village... Clearly there's something in the water around here; there's certainly plenty of it.

Top: **Colourful Upper Kirkgate terrace.**
Left: **Lower Kirkgate.**

St Joseph's RC Church

Derwent Bridge

Old Toll Cottage

Buttermere valley

Bigamy, beer and nowt but scenery

The Buttermere valley is around eight miles long, becoming more dramatic as it unfolds from the flat meadows of Lorton, south of Cockermouth, to the high ground around Great Gable. It is blessed with three lakes – Buttermere, Crummock Water and, just off the main valley, Loweswater – strung together like jewels on a necklace of rivers. The hamlet of Buttermere lies between the two southernmost lakes.

Scenically, the valley is up there with Ullswater and Borrowdale. It's also strikingly uneven in the number of visitors it attracts.

▶ My father used to say: "There's nowt but scenery at Buttermere." I didn't agree with him on much, but thought this statement might be an exception. However, I realised later that he considered 'scenery' a negative quality, whereas I thought the opposite. …So really we didn't agree on anything.

Left: Lorton 'Fishermen's' cottages.

BUTTERMERE

Buttermere is justifiably the prime attraction, with Crummock Water drawing the Lakeland connoisseur – someone who can enjoy the scenery without the need for an accompanying beer, slice of carrot cake or ice cream. Loweswater, meanwhile, is secreted away in a hidden valley, shy of visitors but bountiful to those who treat it with respect.

I first became familiar with Buttermere during school geography, where it was taught as the perfect example of an alluvial plain. The two lakes, Buttermere and Crummock Water, were gouged out of the mountains by glacial action to considerable depths – 94ft and 144ft respectively.

Lorton

Lorton is a scattered village split into High and Low parts, neither of which has an obvious centre. Lorton was an agricultural settlement until the 19th century, when it enjoyed a prosperous period thanks to the textile industry. It's now largely a commuter and holiday village.

Below: The head of Crummock Water looking to High Crag, Warnscale Bottom and Haystacks.

LOWESWATER

The village hall in High Lorton was once the malthouse of the original Jennings Brewery, established in 1828. The company moved to a larger site at Cockermouth in 1874. Nearby cottages, dating to the early 1800s, were once part of the brewery and have steps up to the front doors, like houses around fishing harbours. They're now holiday lets.

Loweswater

This tiny community is linked to the outside world by a narrow, tree-lined road that appears to be going nowhere and takes its time doing so. Adding to the confusion, when the trees do eventually clear, the sensational view that opens up is not of Loweswater as you might expect; it's actually of Crummock Water as viewed from the hamlet of Loweswater.

But no matter – what a view! The reason it might look familiar is that it has appeared on numerous postcards, calendars and coffee table glossies over the years. Grasmoor and Mellbreak buttress an expansive skyline like a pair of bookends, with the big beasts around Buttermere – Robinson, Brandreth, distant Gable – poking their tops above Rannerdale Knotts.

There is no village of Loweswater, only a little community scattered around the rolling fields and coppices between the two lakes. Its centre is the Church of St Bartholomew, the Kirkstile Inn across the road and the former school house – now the village hall – a few yards up the hill.

▼ Lorton Village Shop – also known as 'The shed with a view' – is an admirable enterprise packed with goods ranging from food, coffee and crafts to hiking supplies. It supports over 80 local businesses and has become an unmissable tourist stopping point.

Grasmoor
2,791ft (851m)

Whiteless Pike
2,159ft (658m)

Robinson
2,417ft (737m)

Rannerdale Knotts
1,160ft (354m)

Crummock Water

St Bartholomew's Church

Whiteless Breast

LOWESWATER

▲ A large and scraggy yew tree has stood on the banks of Whit Beck for at least 1,000 years. Both George Fox, the founder of the Quaker movement, and John Wesley, who established the Methodists, stood beneath the tree and preached to large crowds. William Wordsworth wrote a poem about it called 'Yew-Trees'. Soon after, a storm reduced the tree's 27ft girth to a mere 13ft, with the wood of the broken half used to make the Cockermouth mayoral chair.

▲ The Kirkstile Inn in Loweswater is a welcoming 16th-century hostelry with beams and country furnishings. Beers were brewed on site until 2003, before operations moved to a bigger, custom-built brewery in Hawkshead. Cumbrian Ales' award-winning beers are now available all over the Lakes. Supping a Loweswater Gold ('World famous Golden Ale with a tropical fruit flavour') while watching the sun set over Mellbreak is as good as it gets.

Below: Crummock Water from Loweswater village hall.

Mellbreak
1,676ft (511m)

Brandreth
344ft (714m)

Great Gable
2,949ft (899m)

High Stile
2,644ft (806m)

Green Gable
2,603ft (793m)

Haystacks
1,900ft (580m)

Kirkstile Inn

LOWESWATER

Above: **Loweswater from the southern shore.**

A mile or so further on from the hamlet of Loweswater is one of the region's smallest, shallowest and least-known lakes. Loweswater's uniqueness is that it's the only lake whose waters flow inwards to the centre of Lakeland (into Crummock Water) rather than outwards to the sea.

Its diminutive size – just over a mile long, not quite a mile across and with an average depth of around 60ft – makes it one of the first lakes to freeze in winter. You can walk all the way round it, and the heavily wooded south shore abounds with red squirrels and a bounty of wildflowers.

Loweswater is undoubtably pretty, but for me it's the seclusion so close to tourist hotspots that makes it so appealing.

> **❝ It took me years to discover Loweswater and I'm glad I waited until I was old enough to appreciate its gentle charms.**

There are many places in Lakeland where you can find solitude, but often it's the harshness of a locality that keeps people away. Here at Loweswater there's a sylvan beauty that's welcoming to anyone who has the sensitivity to appreciate it. There's nothing showy or dramatic here, but that's part of the appeal.

Young people, hungry for adrenaline, might consider Loweswater to be an old folks' lake; a place for those with time to enjoy a gentle four-mile stroll around shingle shores after a heavy Sunday lunch.

They would probably be right. It took me years to discover Loweswater, and I'm glad I waited until I was old enough to appreciate its gentle charms.

CRUMMOCK WATER

Crummock Water

As the narrow road heads south and the steep and craggy side of Whiteside rises dramatically in the east, one of Lakeland's most striking and evocative views of the Buttermere fells and Crummock Water is revealed. There's a gate beside a small wood that I like to lean on like a proper country gent to bask in its splendour.

Bracken and gorse clothe the skirts of Grasmoor and a band of meadows roll down to the lake beneath Rannerdale Knotts, the great rock barrier to upper Buttermere. For many years the only access to the head of the valley was to climb over it. A road was eventually carved out of the rock face at Hause Point, headland of the Knotts.

Crummock Water is around two and a half miles long, less than a mile across and 144ft deep. It's bigger than Buttermere, but considerably less busy. The narrow, half-mile strip of farmland between the two lakes suggests that at one time they formed a single stretch of water.

I've never been a fan of Crummock Water, finding the long side of Mellbreak across the lake featureless and oppressive. Maybe I should take a walk along the western side of the lake that so many of its devotees rave about.

For me Crummock only comes alive when you round Hause Point and the magnificent mountainscape of upper Buttermere appears out of the mist.

Below: **The view south from Low Wood.**

Rannerdale Knotts 1,160ft (353m)
High Crag 2,443ft (745m)
High Stile 2,644ft (806m)
Bleaberry Combe
Red Pike 2,479ft (756m)
Dodd
Hause Point
Crummock Water

BUTTERMERE

Buttermere

Only a mile and a quarter long and less than half a mile wide, Buttermere is small. But at 75ft it's also deep by Cumbrian standards. A lack of organic material keeps the water clear, while sediment from Honister slate quarry enhances the fabulous reflections with a unique greenish quality. Buttermere is as pretty as the millions of photographs it has generated, but for me its beauty is outshone by the rugged 2,000ft-high (610m) ramparts of the High Stile range towering over the water. Buttermere has other fine fells, but they're no match for these neighbours.

A popular family walk goes around the lake starting from the Buttermere or Gatesgarth car parks. Part of the route goes through a tunnel dug by gardeners at nearby Hassness House, allegedly to give them something to do during the winter. As a family we've walked around the lake a few times – even climbed up Scarth Gap to Haystacks and looked down the valley to secretive Ennerdale Water. I've yet to complete the classic high level circuit of Red Pike, High Stile and High Crag, and fear it may now be too late.

Left: The head of Buttermere and the famous pine trees.
Below: Buttermere village.

BUTTERMERE

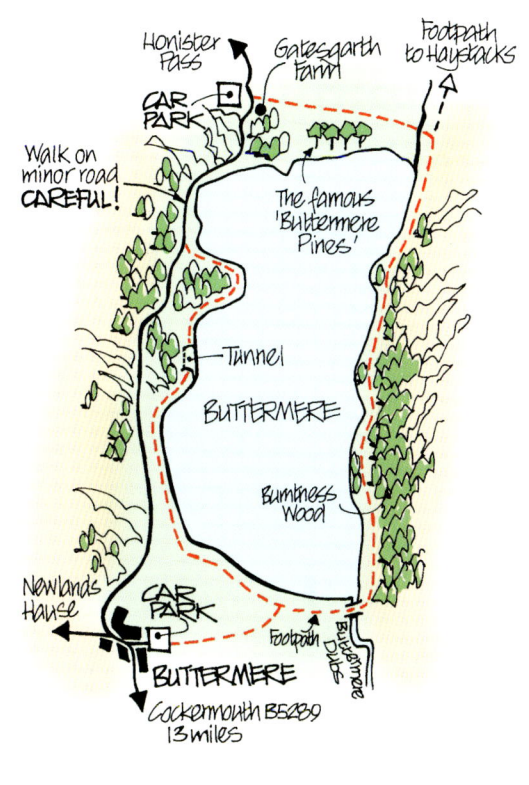

▲ The tiny Church of St James was built in 1840 on a rocky perch above the village. Twin bells hang in the bell turret and the wrought-iron porch gate depicts a hill shepherd and his sheep. Inside, 16 carved angels gaze down from the ceiling. One of the windows contains a plaque in memory of Alfred Wainwright urging visitors to 'Lift your eyes to Haystacks / His favourite place'. After his death in 1991, the fellwalker's ashes were scattered near the summit of the fell.

Without the crowds (and its two pubs and various eateries) Buttermere is one of those hamlets you could conceivably walk through without realising you'd arrived. Nevertheless, it's a splendid centre for exploring, with a beautiful setting, two fine lakes within strolling distance, grand fell walks and iconic rock climbs for the enthusiasts.

No wonder it often gets over-busy, with car parks overflowing and vehicles abandoned along the roadside spreading far up the hill towards Newlands Hause… All at ten o'clock in the morning.

▲ Syke Farm is one of the Buttermere farmsteads that has diversified into hospitality. Their tearoom serves farmhouse-style food with a variety of home-made cakes and scrumptious lunches. More importantly, they also make the best ice cream in the district, using milk from the cows that graze the meadows below the farm.

BUTTERMERE

In 1802, the tabloids of the time went into overdrive when Mary Robinson, the beautiful daughter of the landlord of Buttermere's Fish Inn, was tricked into marriage by a conman and bigamist calling himself the Honourable Alexander Hope. His real name was John Hatfield, and he had both a wife and children.

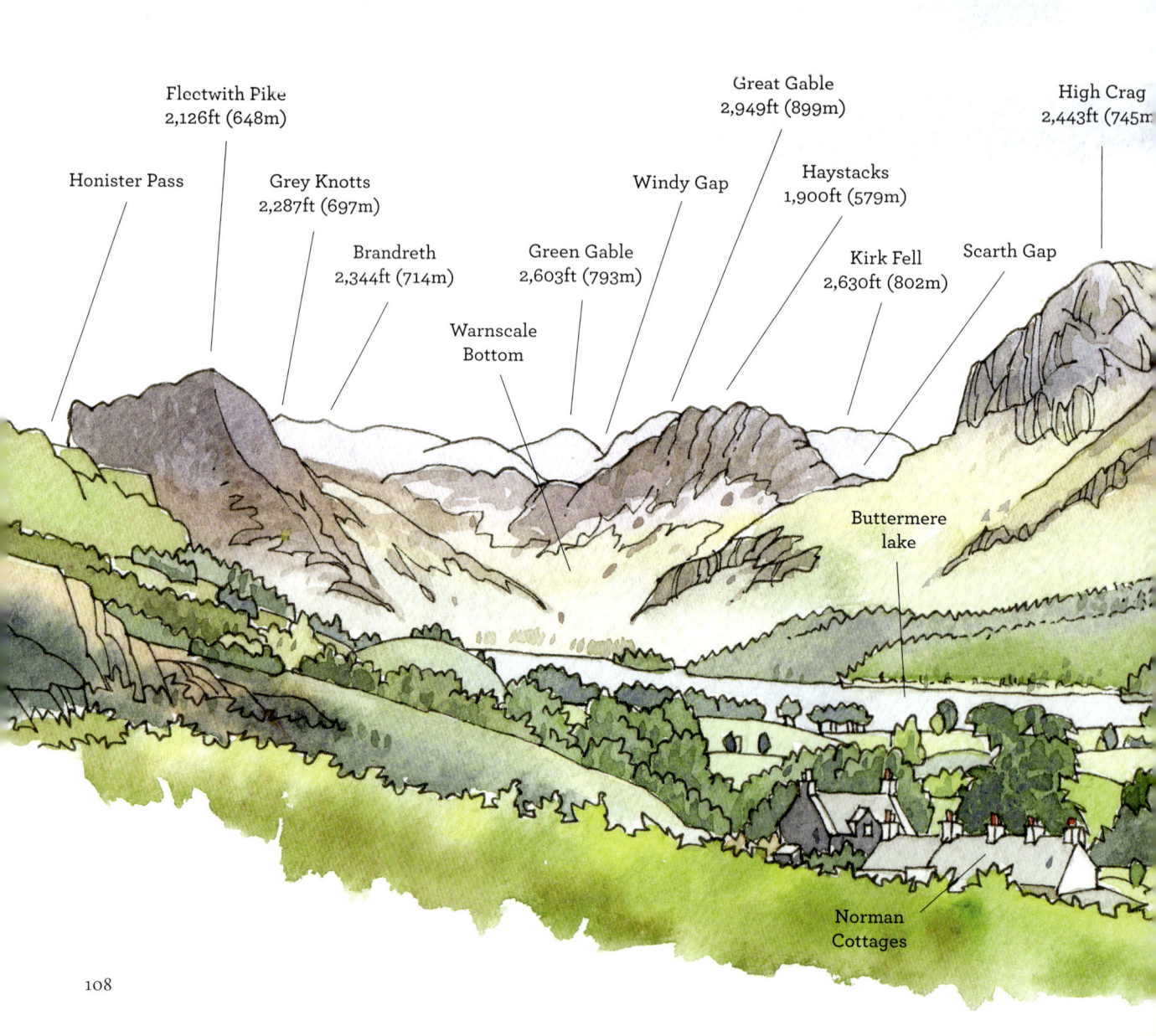

- Honister Pass
- Fleetwith Pike 2,126ft (648m)
- Grey Knotts 2,287ft (697m)
- Brandreth 2,344ft (714m)
- Warnscale Bottom
- Green Gable 2,603ft (793m)
- Great Gable 2,949ft (899m)
- Windy Gap
- Haystacks 1,900ft (579m)
- Kirk Fell 2,630ft (802m)
- Scarth Gap
- High Crag 2,443ft (745m)
- Buttermere lake
- Norman Cottages

BUTTERMERE

He was unmasked by the local gentry, tried for franking his mail as a bogus member of Parliament and hanged at Carlisle a year later.

Mary, the so-called 'Maid of Buttermere', had plays and songs written about her – even Wordsworth mentioned her in 'The Prelude' – and visitors flocked to The Fish to catch a glimpse of the unfortunate girl. More recently, in 1987, Melvyn Bragg wrote a novel based on her story.

Mary later married a Caldbeck farmer, Richard Harrison, and lived the remains of her life in relative peace. She died in 1837 after raising four children.

Far left: **The Fish Inn.**
Below: **The head of Buttermere from the slopes of Low Bank.**

Bassenthwaite
& Back o' Skiddaw

The only lake, a pub song hit and a tearful visit

BASSENTHWAITE

As local wags have it, Bassenthwaite is the only true 'lake' in the Lake District; all the others are 'meres' or 'waters'. At four miles long, just under a mile wide and with a maximum depth of 70ft, it's certainly one of the largest. Set furthest north, if you travel beyond the lake you leave Lakeland. The difference in landscape is both sudden and noticeable – and for a sentimentalist like me often a bit sad.

Part of the A66 follows the route of the much-lamented Penrith to Cockermouth railway line along the lakeside; what a visitor attraction that would have been today.

There's no real settlement at the lakeside – even the village is more than a mile from its banks – so the lake is a peaceful outpost and, except for the heavy A66 traffic along the west side, relatively unspoilt. *The Guardian* newspaper once went way over the top and named Bassenthwaite one of "the best lakes to visit in Europe". What the criteria were wasn't spelt out.

It is possible to walk most of the way around the lake except for the wildlife reserve at the southern end and a stretch of lakeshore around Mirehouse country house. Access to the lake is only available there if you pay to visit the house. The fell views along both the east and west sides are superb, with Skiddaw dominating the scene.

Towering over the Swan Hotel at Thornthwaite, Barf is a fearsome pyramid of a fell described by Wainwright as one no passer-by would dream of climbing from this steep eastern approach.

Alas, legend has it that in order to prove his faith in God a bishop once did – while riding his horse! It must have been God's day off, as both horse and bishop fell and died. A small rock pinnacle on the fellside is said to mark the extent of their ascent. Traditionally painted white by the landlord of the Swan, the 'Bishop of Barf' is a popular landmark that can be seen from miles around.

While researching my *Guide to the Allerdale Ramble* on a bright summer's morning in 1995, I embarked on an ascent of Skiddaw, going straight up the hillside from Millbeck.

At the summit of Carl Side, after surveying the forbidding scree slope that rises up to Skiddaw summit, I decided to take the more attractive route alternative and cross the narrow ridge to Ullock Pike and descend The Edge to Bassenthwaite.

It was a good choice. With the sparkling lake below me on the south side and the barren depths of Southerndale on the north it was an unforgettable descent.

> **"** *The Guardian* newspaper once went way over the top and named Bassenthwaite one of "the best lakes to visit in Europe".

Far left: Bassenthwaite Lake and Skiddaw.
Left: The Bishop of Barf.
Below: Bassenthwaite Lake, with Skiddaw beyond.

BASSENTHWAITE

Above: Central Bassenthwaite.

Bassenthwaite

With a green, a pub and ducks on the river flowing through it, Bassenthwaite is the archetypal English village. But this being the Lake District, there are also three farms in the village and many of the houses are barn conversions, holiday lets and second homes. An avenue of fine trees across a green make a grand entrance from the south and a stroll around the maze of narrow streets is an excellent way to work up a thirst for a drink at the Sun Inn.

In 2001 a pair of ospreys nested near Bassenthwaite Lake, the first pair to do so for at least 150 years. Every year since the birds have made the 3,000-mile journey back from Africa to nest and raise their young. They usually arrive in April, the eggs hatch in June and then the adults and chicks head back to Africa in September.

The Lake District Osprey Project operates a viewpoint at the Forestry Commission's Dodd Wood, near Keswick, from where the nest can be viewed through high-powered telescopes from a safe distance. You can also watch the birds on the nest-cam at Whinlatter Forest Centre.

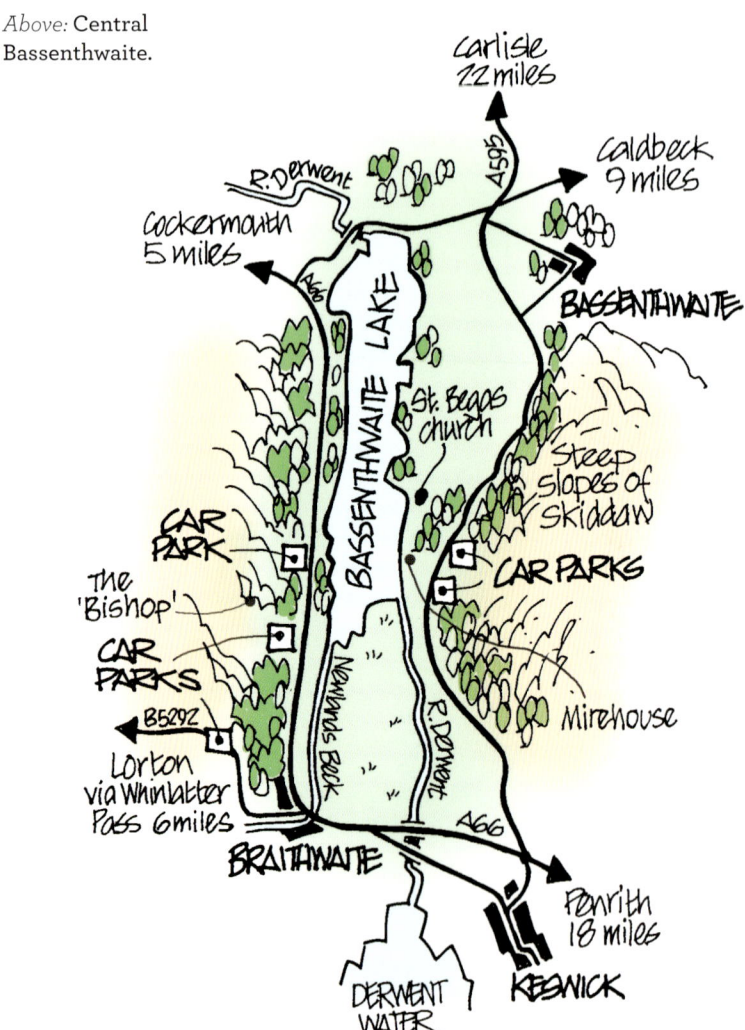

BASSENTHWAITE

It's interesting – although at times it feels a bit like watching a David Attenborough nature programme without his commentary, music, and needle-sharp, much-enhanced photography.

St Bega's Church occupies an idyllic and isolated situation on the east shore of Bassenthwaite Lake and can only be reached on foot. The building dates from around AD950, though the site may be older, and it was extensively restored in 1874. Christian worship has taken place here for over 1,000 years and people travel from all over the world to sample its serene and mystical atmosphere. The church interior is beautifully maintained and is always open.

Melvyn Bragg used St Bega's as the setting for his Anglo-Celtic epic *Credo,* and Bassenthwaite Lake is said to have moved Tennyson to write his lines about Excalibur when he was staying at Mirehouse.

Still hard at work on *Ramble* research, I wandered along the lakeshore on a bright summer's morning without seeing a soul. St Bega's drew me in and I sat in a pew for a while, absorbing the rarified atmosphere.

After a few minutes I began to cry. I'm not religious, but silent old churches do have this effect on me. Dramatic lighting across Lakeland scenes and pieces of music set me off too. How teary I get is a measure of the quantity of emotion I'm experiencing – a bit like the Beaufort Scale for wind speed.

When I rejoined the real world on Bassenthwaite lakeside, still drenched in mystic romanticism, I fully expected to see an arm reaching out of the lake clutching a glittering sword.

If it had, my Blubbing Scale would surely have hit maximum.

Above: St Bega's Church.

> **❝** After a few minutes I began to cry. I'm not religious, but silent old churches do have this effect on me.

▼ Built in 1666 by the Earl of Derby, with a majestic setting on the eastern shore of Bassenthwaite, Mirehouse has been the home of the Spedding family since 1802. During the 19th century the family were friends with many of the artistic giants of the day, including Wordsworth, Tennyson, Southey, Thomas Carlyle and John Constable.

James Spedding, a noted 19th-century literary figure, spent most of his life writing a 14-volume biography of Francis Bacon. His father, John, also had literary connections, having spent six years as a classmate of William Wordsworth at Hawkshead Grammar School. Some of Wordsworth's letters are on display in the house.

Over the years Mirehouse has been adapted for several households to live in, but much of the house – and the private lake shore – is now open to the paying public.

113

ULDALE

Uldale

Uldale is a typical north Lakes village built amongst rolling hills on the fringe of the National Park. There are a few farms and old cottages converted to desirable residences and B&Bs. The Snooty Fox pub caters for locals and passing tourist trade.

A Norse-Irish settlement existed here in the ninth century, the name Uldale deriving from the Norse word for 'wolf' – recalling the days when wolves roamed the fells around here in abundance. A farming area since medieval times, a sheep fair was established in the village in 1791. Abandoned copper and limestone quarries offer evidence of 19th-century mining in the area between the village and Caldbeck.

Uldale was the setting for David's house in Hugh Walpole's *Herries Chronicle*. Indeed, much of the village and its surroundings feature in both *Judith Paris* and *The Fortress*. Huntsman John Peel spent the latter part of his life here after marrying Uldale girl Mary White.

The last time I was in Uldale we stopped on the steep hill above the village to watch flocks of geese cackling across from the Solway Firth towards Bassenthwaite – a great sight, especially with an uninterrupted view to the glittering Solway and Scottish hills beyond.

The road climbs out of the village then crosses a cattle-grid into an area of unfenced moorland that Walt Unsworth, founder of Cicerone publishers, once described as "one of the true wilderness areas of the Lake District".

Above: Uldale.
Below: The Snooty Fox.

BACK O' SKIDDAW

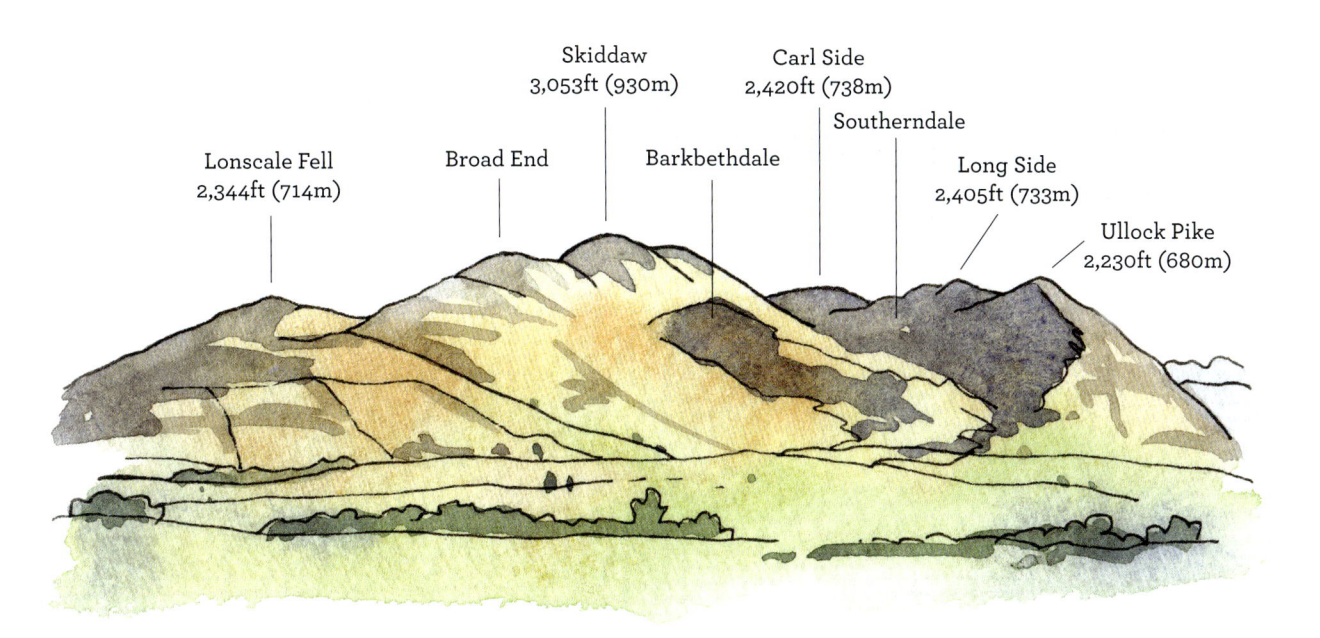

Lonscale Fell 2,344ft (714m)
Broad End
Skiddaw 3,053ft (930m)
Barkbethdale
Carl Side 2,420ft (738m)
Southerndale
Long Side 2,405ft (733m)
Ullock Pike 2,230ft (680m)

Above: **Skiddaw from Uldale.**
Below: **Approaching Over Water.**

The Caldbeck and Uldale fells are generally featureless; this is a world of moorland grass and scattered farms that receives few visitors. Walkers who prefer a more craggy landscape have been known to unkindly call this area the 'Back o' Beyond'. Yet there's a lot to be said for solitude – and I often say it.

However, the actual Back o' Skiddaw (or to be strictly accurate, the *Side* o' Skiddaw) is a fine sight from Uldale, with the long ridge of Ullock Pike and Long Side curving dramatically down to Bassenthwaite, revealing the reclusive valleys of Barkbethdale and Southerndale.

There are many surprises in this area, but probably none as stark as Over Water, a small lake set amongst fields along a back road from Uldale.

Originally a remote stretch of water with the Norse name of Orre Water, it was dammed in 1904 to provide water for the town of Wigton, some eight miles north. Notable as a feeding ground for the Bassenthwaite ospreys, it is owned by the National Trust, and is private.

CALDBECK

Above: Cottages along the River Caldew.
Below: The former brewery and mill buildings.

Caldbeck

One of my favourite Lakeland villages, Caldbeck lies in a limestone basin hard up against the northern fells on the edge of the National Park. It's peaceful and residential, with a pretty river and some fine houses – legacies of the village's former wealth, accumulated when Caldbeck was one of Cumberland's great mining centres.

The Caldbeck fells have been extensively mined since Elizabethan times. The industry's most spectacular growth was in the 18th and 19th centuries when 14 mines – mainly yielding silver, copper and lead – were sunk into the fells above the village. Digging the ore must have been punishing enough – but the miners then had to carry it over ten miles of bleak fellside to be smelted at Keswick.

The village prospered with more than a dozen mills and a brewery along the River Caldew. Coal for local use was mined within the village itself from shallow pits on Ratten Row, which fringes the village green. With the population mushrooming to more than 1,500 (and with 13 alehouses) it must have been a busy – and boisterous – place to live. The last mine closed in 1965 and just one pub remains.

Standing near the bridge over the Caldew at the southern end of the village green, the brewery and Lord's Mill have been turned into desirable private houses. The brewery was formerly a wheat mill dating back to 1670. Brewing began in 1810 and ceased along with the industrial boom at the end of the 19th century. Lord's Mill, still with its checker-brick chimney, ground corn from 1704 to 1914.

CALDBECK

Gate House, the former home of John Graves

D'ye ken John Peel?

In the centre of Caldbeck, 12th-century St Kentigern's Church attracts visitors to the grave of John Peel, the Lakeland hunter of foxes immortalised in song.

Peel was born in 1776 at Parkend, near Caldbeck. He married the daughter of a well-off farmer who bore him 13 children. Family man he wasn't, however, and he spent most of his time hunting or singing ditties in the pub.

A farmer by profession, Peel kept his own pack of fox hounds and hunted on foot in the Cumbrian fashion – necessary considering the fellside territory the hunt covered.

In 1829, one of his boozing pals, John Graves, wrote some words about him, which, set to a popular Scottish folk tune, were sung in Caldbeck pub The Oddfellows.

Graves owned a local woollen mill which produced the heavy cloth of Peel's 'coat so grey' – not 'coat so gay' as it's sometimes sung. When his mill fell on hard times, Graves left his wife to lead the life of a ne'er-do-well in Tasmania, where he died in 1886.

The choirmaster of Carlisle Cathedral, William Metcalf, gave Graves' song a new tune in 1869, and, after it was sung in London, 'D'ye Ken John Peel?' became a hit.

Above: The Oddfellows.
Below: St Kentigern's Church.

Aged 78, Peel died of a hunting accident in 1854, with thousands turning out for his funeral. His ornate white headstone in the churchyard also carries the names of his long-suffering wife, Mary (who lived to the ripe old age of 82), as well as four of his children.

Less easy to find is the resting place of Mary Harrison – the Maid of Buttermere, who settled in Caldbeck after earning unwanted notoriety at the hands of journalists, poets and scores of Lakeland visitors (*page 106*).

CALDBECK

Above: Priest's Mill.

Caldbeck welcomes visitors and they are well catered for, but the village character hasn't been overwhelmed by tourism – there's even free parking near the river.

Hesta Scene is an alternative gift shop and gallery situated in the Tithe Barn next to the village store. It sells local hand-made items for the home. Whenever we go in, we always end up buying something.

The village layout makes it ideal for a circular walk. From the lovely stone bridge behind the church, a short pathway along the river goes to Priest's Mill, built on the Caldew in 1701 by the rector. It's now converted into three craft workshops and has an excellent tearoom and restaurant, The Watermill Café, overlooking the village cricket field.

▲ Just upstream along the Caldew there's a ruined bobbin mill with a date stone of 1857 and two beautiful arched doorways. The wood drying shed still stands, but the 42ft-diameter waterwheel – once the largest in Britain – was scrapped during the war effort of 1940. At one time 60 men and boys worked here. Closure came in 1920.

Nearby is 'The Howk', where the river has formed a spectacular gorge in the limestone with two deep holes, The Fairy Keetle and The Fairy Kirk, where the water spins and froths. The romantic Victorians gathered here for picnics, with the local paper printing weather forecasts and likely condition of the water flow.

HESKET NEWMARKET

Above: The village of Hesket Newmarket.
Above right: The Old Crown.

Hesket Newmarket

A couple of miles away – and closely bound with Caldbeck – the hamlet of Hesket Newmarket is a picturesque gem of mainly 18th-century houses clustered around a five-acre village green and market cross.

A market charter was awarded in the 18th century, but Hesket never caught on as a market town and by the end of the 19th century the 'newmarket' had closed.

The village shop is at the heart of the community, with a post office and popular tearoom. It sells the products of some 30 local suppliers including honey, pies, sausages and ready meals.

The Old Crown overlooking the green was Britain's first co-operative pub, bought by 150 local residents in 2003. A thriving microbrewery behind the pub is also owned by a collective, formed in 1999. Its famous beers such as Skiddaw Special and Doris' 90th Birthday Ale are sold across a wide area. The mountaineer Sir Chris Bonington lives nearby, as did his fellow climber, Doug Scott, until his death in 2020. Another of the remote hamlet's claims to fame is that the haulage empire of Eddie Stobart began in a Hesket Newmarket back yard. Yes, really!

▲ Hesket Hall, a prominent square house at the top end of the village, was built around 1630 for Sir Wilfrid Lawson, twice MP for Cockermouth. The shape of the house is all angles and annexes; it is said to be so that shadows from the 12 corners of the building would act as a sundial.

Grasmere & Thirlmere

Poetry, puzzles and Mancunian thirst

The best-known, most visited, and most revered of all Lakeland villages, Grasmere sits regally in a lush bowl of fells, overlooked to the north by Helm Crag and edged by the pretty lake in the south which shares the village name. Seen in autumn colours from Loughrigg Terrace you can see why Wordsworth called it "the loveliest spot that man hath ever found".

Below: **Grasmere from Loughrigg Terrace.**

A grey slate collection of hotels, gift shops and cafés – as well as a strong and occasionally vocal community – Grasmere is never going to rival its surroundings in a beauty contest, but it is a pleasant enough tourist honeypot. The River Rothay meanders through the village and an inspired footpath follows it linking two car parks, one at each end of the village.

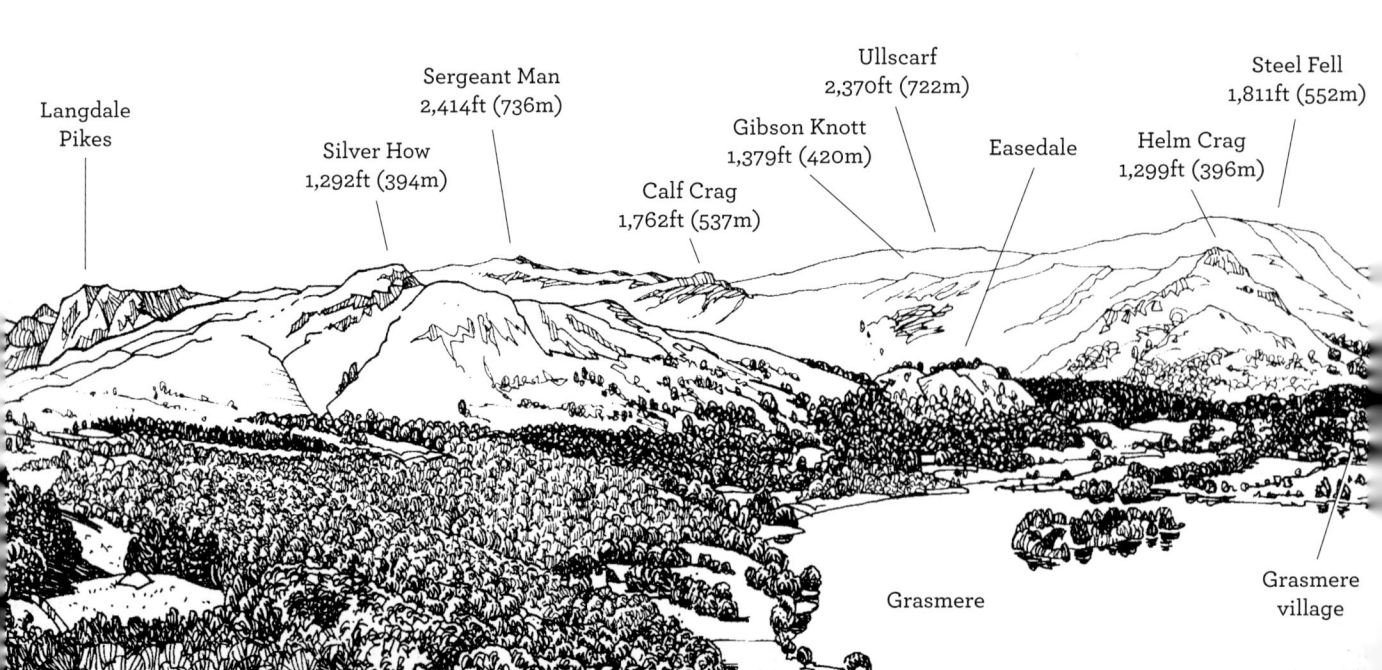

Langdale Pikes

Silver How
1,292ft (394m)

Sergeant Man
2,414ft (736m)

Calf Crag
1,762ft (537m)

Gibson Knott
1,379ft (420m)

Ullscarf
2,370ft (722m)

Easedale

Helm Crag
1,299ft (396m)

Steel Fell
1,811ft (552m)

Grasmere

Grasmere village

GRASMERE

I can't remember when I first visited Grasmere; it just seems always to have been there. My relationship with the village remains ambivalent to this day – we don't rush to visit, although we inevitably get there at some point.

The romantic popularisation of Grasmere began with the Lake Poets, and specifically with the village's most famous literary lion, William Wordsworth. He was a true Cumbrian, born in Cockermouth, schooled at Hawkshead and resident of the Rothay valley in various houses for over 50 years until his death in 1850.

The Wordsworth Museum at Town End attracts tourists and scholars from all over the world, and the £3m Wordsworth Trust Research Centre dedicated to the study of Wordsworth and British Romanticism opened nearby in 2005.

Above: **Helm Crag beyond Grasmere.**

onscale Fell
344ft (714m)

Dunmail Raise

Seat Sandal
2,415ft (736m)

Dollywaggon Pike
2,810ft (856m)

White Moss

Great Rigg
2,513ft (766m)

Heron Pike
2,003ft (610m)

Nab Scar

Rydal Water

GRASMERE

The Wordsworth houses

William and his sister Dorothy moved into Dove Cottage, a former inn, in 1799. The poet married Mary Hutchinson in 1802, a childhood friend who bore him five children, three of them born here. Sara, Mary's sister, later also joined them, and with a frequent flow of visitors – including fellow Lake Poets Coleridge and Southey – the tiny seven-roomed cottage was often very overcrowded.

These days Dove Cottage is the principal Wordsworth shrine, attracting thousands of tourists and scholars each year. I like the fact that it still looks like an ordinary house thanks to the Trust's canny promotion of the Wordsworth philosophy of 'plain living and high thinking'.

After eight happy years at Dove Cottage, during which William wrote many of his greatest works, the Wordsworths relocated to Allan Bank, a large house on the lower slopes of Helm Crag.

Despite its location, William disliked the house, complaining about the extra expense and its smoking chimneys. In time, he came to refer to it as a "temple of abomination".

Above: **Dove Cottage.**
Below left: **Allan Bank.**
Below right: **The Old Parsonage.**

After two years at Allan Bank the family moved down the road to the Old Parsonage. This was another disastrous move; two of the Wordsworths' children, Thomas (aged six) and Catherine (three), died there. Mortified, in 1813 the family left Grasmere for Rydal Mount, two miles away.

GRASMERE

▶ When in Grasmere, I like to call in at the Heaton Cooper Gallery to marvel at the paintings. William Heaton Cooper (1903–95) was an impressionistic watercolour artist who depicted the Lakes in all seasons. The excellent Mathilde's Café attached is named after Cooper's Norwegian mother. My wife Maureen, a jigsaw enthusiast, loves Barney's Newsbox, just down the road. It's a veritable mecca for fans of the genre.

◀ Externally St Oswald's Church has a grey, sombre look, but inside it's surprisingly bright and beautiful. The earliest parts of the building date back to the 13th century and the lower walls are four feet thick.

The early church had an earthen floor covered with rushes from the lake side which, until 1841 when the floor was flagged, were renewed at least once a year. The custom survives in the annual Rushbearing Ceremony, which is held on the nearest Saturday to St Oswald's Day (5 August).

The Wordsworths were regular worshippers at St Oswald's and 15 of the extended family are buried in the churchyard.

▶ The Gingerbread Shop is part of the old Grasmere entrance to the churchyard and used to be the village schoolroom, built in 1687. Sarah Nelson first made her spicy, crumbly Grasmere Gingerbread in this room after it was let to her in 1854.

Despite it having worldwide fans, I prefer the gingerbread my mother used to make: soft and cake-like with a spread of butter on top. It was the perfect teatime treat.

GRASMERE

Above: Boat landings on Grasmere.
Opposite: Grasmere from the corpse road.

Grasmere is one of Lakeland's smaller lakes, being around just one mile long, a half-mile wide and with a maximum depth of 70ft. A weir at the outlet to Rydal Water maintains its water level. The wooded island on the lake is known simply as 'The Island' – a rather prosaic name for a place so rich in poetic romanticism. Apart from the Daffodil Hotel at Town End, there are no buildings on the lakeside, though rowing boats can be hired.

At the end of 2019, the owners of the lake, Lowther Estates, announced plans to float ten holiday houseboats on it. After a national outcry and string of local protests, the plan was withdrawn in early 2020.

Visitors fresh off tour coaches in the village can often be seen puzzling over how to access the lake. It's complicated: you either have to backtrack along the busy A591, or, better, walk uphill along Red Bank towards Elterwater, then turn left down a footpath to reach the lake shore.

After a blissful stroll by the water, the view back to the village and Helm Crag can be appreciated in all its glory. Set against the wooded fells in autumnal colours or when mist hangs over the water, the scene can be glorious.

> **"** Visitors fresh off tour coaches in the village can often be seen puzzling over how to access the lake.

Rydal Water

Often marketed together as a single tourist destination, Grasmere and Rydal Water are physically linked by a short stretch of the River Rothay meandering gently through White Moss – an area of natural paddling pools, picnic spots and woodland walks. We've spent many happy family times here, and White Moss is the hub for some excellent low-level walks.

Rydal Water is a gem, less than a mile long, 400 yards across and 50ft deep in parts. There are two islands, both thickly crowned with Scots Pines and oaks. Surrounded by low fells and with only one building in sight – Nab Cottage – the lake has a look of remoteness contrary to its physical location less than a mile out of busy Ambleside and with the A591 running alongside it.

Nab Cottage was once the home of Thomas De Quincey, writer and acquaintance of the Lake Poets. He moved into Dove Cottage after the Wordsworths moved out, and then annoyed them when he retained the cottage as a store for his books after relocating to Rydal Water. Dated 1702, Nab Cottage is now a guesthouse.

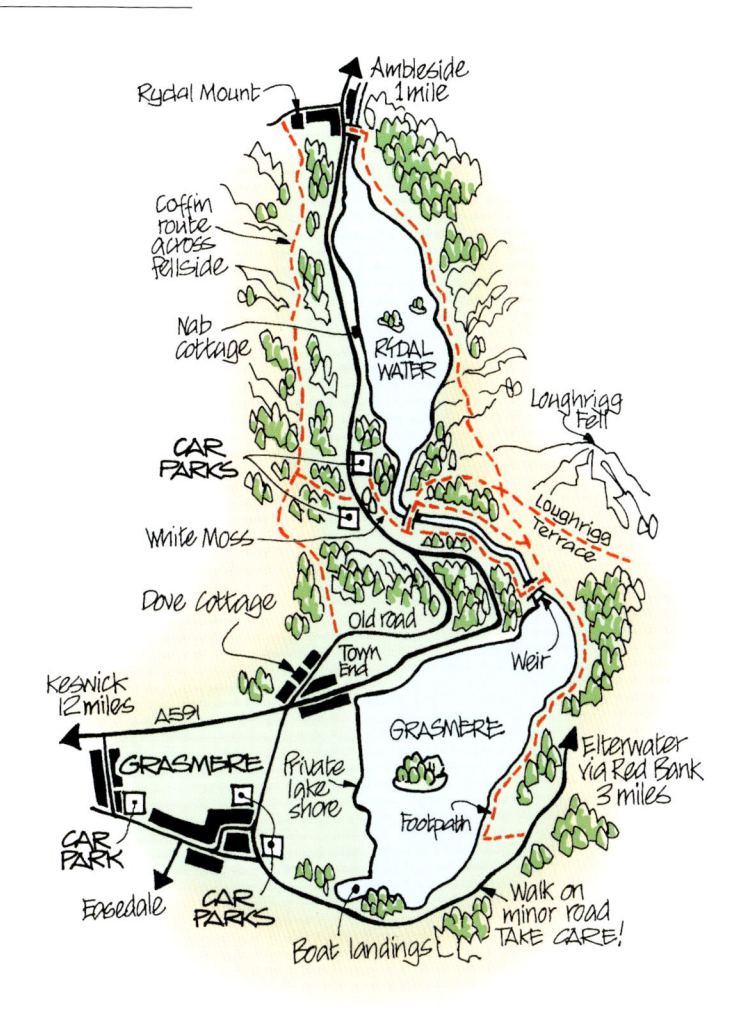

▲ One of our favourite family walks is the classic 'corpse road' circuit of Grasmere and Rydal Water (*mapped in red*), including a noisy visit to the echoing 'cave' on Loughrigg Fell – actually a disused slate quarry. After the predicted moans of "Are we there yet?" on the drag up to Rydal Mount, the coffin route across the fellside is full of interest, with wandering sheep and trees growing out of rocks. This route was a favourite of the Wordsworths, and it's easy to see why: the views over the lake are fabulous all the way and the descent to Townhead and Dove Cottage is magical.

The old road from White Moss to Grasmere is shorter but no less enjoyable, with picnic places and wide views of Rydal Water and its tree-spread surroundings.

RYDAL

Rydal

Traffic pours through Rydal like sand in an egg-timer. A spur of Loughrigg Fell creates a bottleneck between Rydal Water and Ambleside that both the A591 and River Rothay have to squeeze through.

Rydal is a select hamlet of fine houses and cottages spread around the junction of the A591 and a lane that leads up the hill to the big-star residence of Rydal Mount, home of William Wordsworth until his death in 1850. There's a tiny car park for visitors to the Mount. Other motorists cram their vehicles nose-to-tail up the steep lane.

Trees grow in abundance here, soaring up the crag sides and cascading over river and road. Cheerful in sunshine, Rydal turns depressing when it's raining; it can sometimes feel as if Wordsworth's character still haunts the hillsides.

Lady Le Fleming of nearby Rydal Hall built St Mary's Church below Rydal Mount. One of its windows is dedicated to Dr Arnold, head of Rugby School, who once had a holiday house in Rydal Park. The Wordsworths had the best pew in the church – right in front of the pulpit.

Left: **St Mary's Church, Rydal.**
Below: **The view east from White Moss Common.**

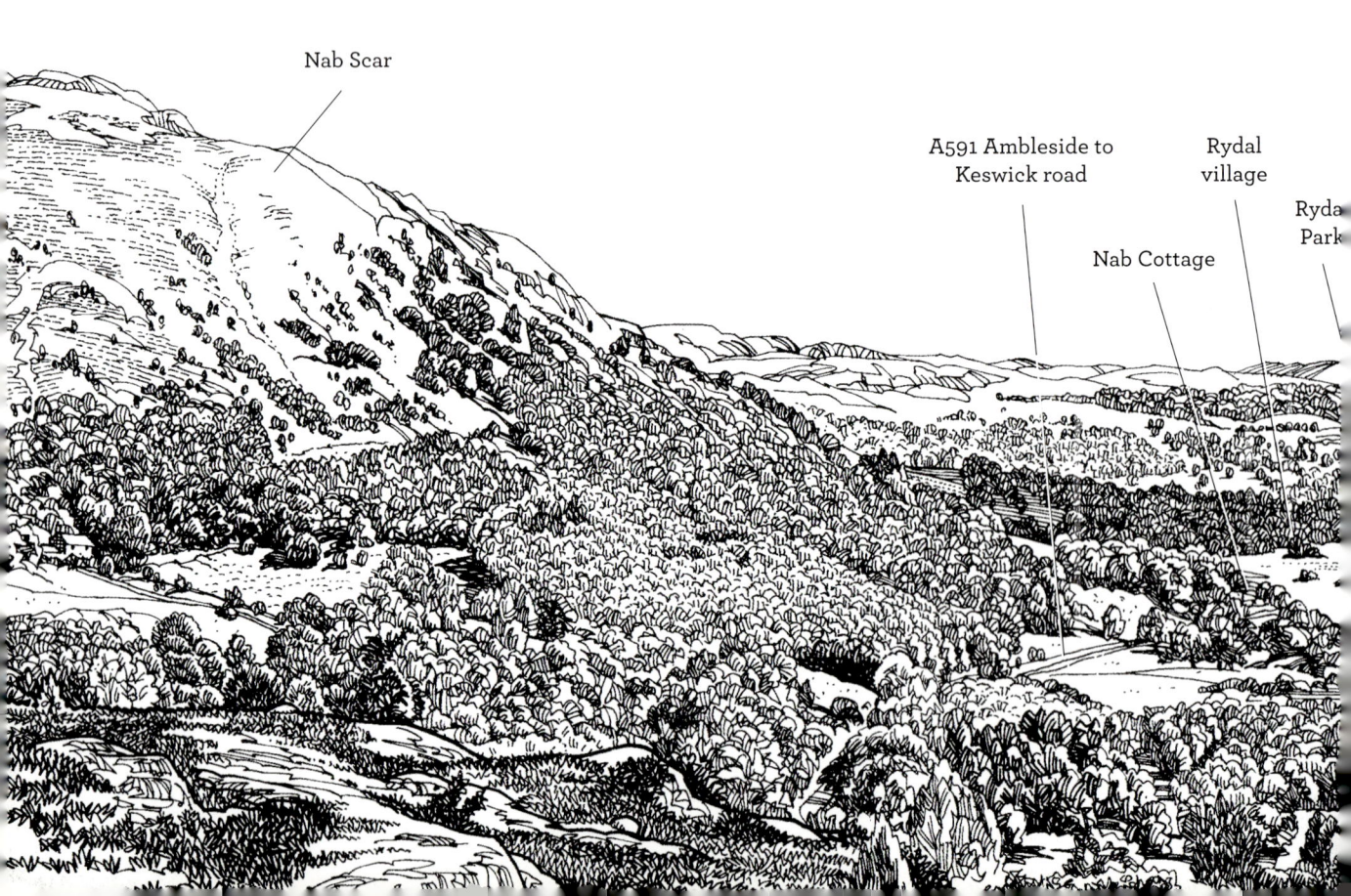

- Nab Scar
- A591 Ambleside to Keswick road
- Rydal village
- Nab Cottage
- Rydal Park

RYDAL

▶ Rydal Mount is a surprisingly light and spacious house, the grandest the Wordsworths lived in and totally different to Dove Cottage. Now owned by a descendant of the poet, and open to the public since 1970, the Mount contains some of Wordsworth's furniture, alongside manuscripts and personal possessions.

Wordsworth landscaped the gardens and dedicated a field at the bottom to his daughter Dora after she died in 1847, aged 43. Bright with a host of daffodils in spring, it's still called Dora's Field.

Wordsworth lived the life of a grand old man of letters with gusto, the cultural greats of the day trudging up the steep lane to pay their respects. Queen Victoria made him Poet Laureate while Lord Lowther elected him Distributer of Stamps for Westmorland – a kind of local tax collector.

The poet died at the age of 80, a legend in his own lifetime and an even bigger one since.

Above: Rydal Mount.

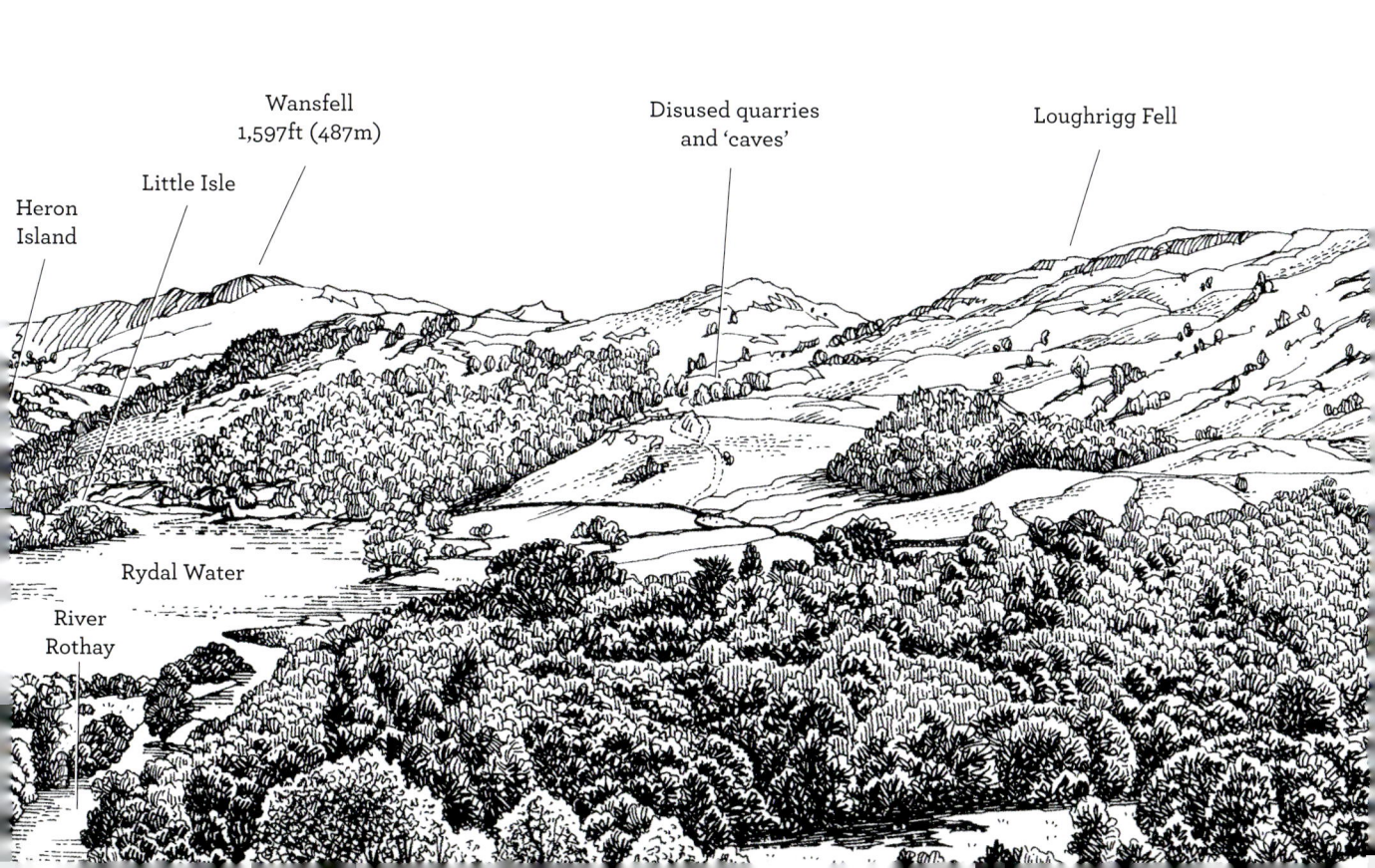

THIRLMERE

Thirlmere

Though often overlooked in the pantheon of Lakeland picturesque on the grounds that it was created by human endeavour – and is thus unnatural – Thirlmere is worth attention as the only significant stretch of water that boasts reflections of the mighty Helvellyn range in its water. It's also a superb example of Victorian civil engineering.

Thirlmere was created from two smaller lakes – Leathes Water and Wythburn Water – by the construction of a dam during 1890–94, to supply water to the city of Manchester via a 100-mile aqueduct. The first pipeline, a single 40-inch-diameter pipe, was turned on in 1894, with the lake level raised 20ft above normal. As the demand for water increased, so did the number of pipes. By 1927 there were four pipes and the water level had been raised 50ft.

The Thirlmere Aqueduct is the longest gravity-fed aqueduct in the country, with no pumps along its route. A tunnel was dug under Dunmail Raise by two teams working towards each other; the tunnels met within ten inches of centre.

▲ Thirlmere is a little over three miles long and just under half a mile wide, with a maximum depth of around 130ft. An outlet flows north along St John's Beck, joining the Glenderamackin at Threlkeld to become the Greta that flows through – and sometimes into – Keswick. Situated at the north end of the lake, the dam is 857ft long and 50ft thick at the bottom, rising 64ft above the old stream bed. The top is 18ft wide and has a road across it.

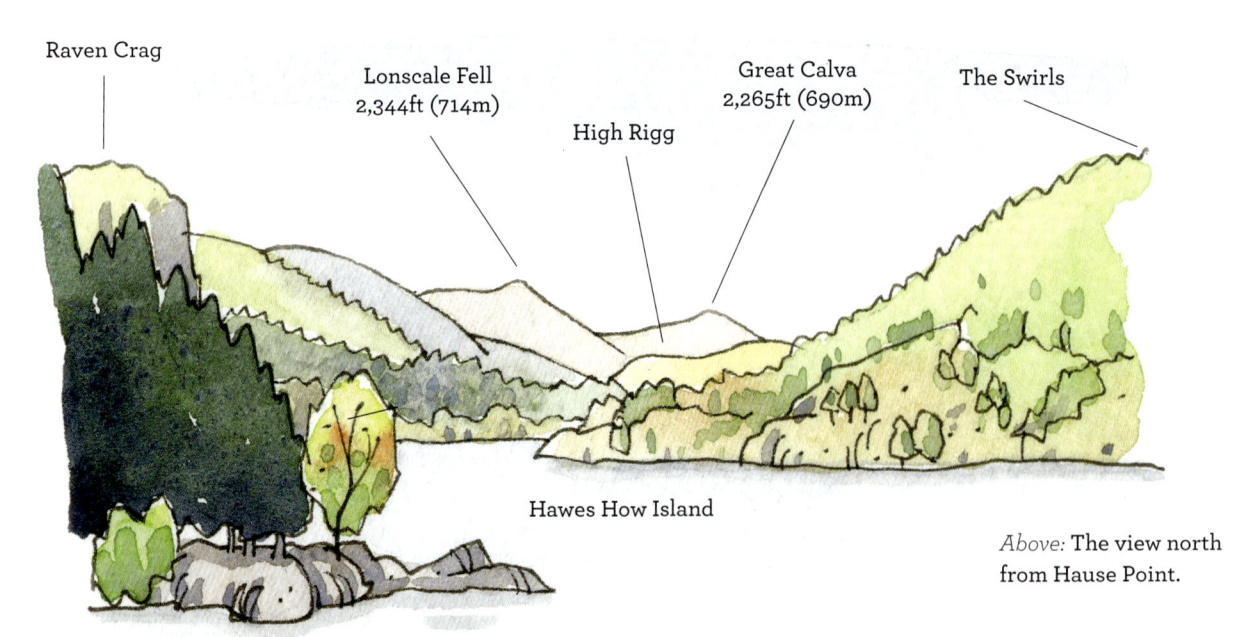

Raven Crag
Lonscale Fell 2,344ft (714m)
High Rigg
Great Calva 2,265ft (690m)
The Swirls
Hawes How Island

Above: **The view north from Hause Point.**

THIRLMERE

The fell sides around the lake were originally planted with 120 acres of conifers as an early cash crop, but the alien trees were widely disliked. Now, thanks to modern forestry management – and persistent campaigning by 67-year-old Susan Johnson, who took North West Water to court in 1985 in a remarkable David vs Goliath fight over tree-planting around the reservoir margins – Thirlmere has a more natural look.

Above: Steel End Farm on the old road at the south end of the lake. It escaped the flooding of the valley.
Below: Blencathra and St John's in the Vale from the Swirls car park.

▲ The tiny church at Wythburn is one of few buildings that survived the raising of the water level. Built in 1640, it was enlarged in 1872. The two inns that used to serve the valley and travellers on the lakeside road are long gone.

Ambleside & the Langdales

Glitterati, gunpowder and moonshine

A bustling town of shops, hotels, guesthouses, pubs and restaurants, superbly set between the head of Windermere and a panorama of shapely fells, Ambleside is the perfect base for exploring central Lakeland. There's everything the visitor needs – except maybe somewhere to park.

Ambleside has long been a popular stopping place for travellers. At the end of the 17th century the town had five alehouses and a weekly market. The arrival of the railway to Windermere in the mid-18th century opened the area to a huge influx of new visitors.

The first outdoor shop in the town opened in 1959 and the number of visitors has grown ever since.

For years I wasn't a fan of Ambleside, regarding it as a necessary hazard to get through on the way to somewhere else. However, when researching my *Lakeland Towns* book in 1987, I found much to enjoy and plenty of interesting scenes to draw.

AMBLESIDE

◄ Ambleside's most iconic building, Bridge House, spans Stock Beck and has survived not only megastardom on calendars and postcards, but also the construction of Rothay Road alongside it in 1833.

Built as an apple store for nearby Ambleside Hall, it's now a cramped National Trust shop. The roof still has original 17th-century 'wrestler slates' along the ridge. The house has had many uses over the years, mainly as a store, but it has also served time as a weaver's workshop, a cobbler's and a tearoom. At one time it was even home to a family of eight.

William Green, a local artist, recorded the rural scene for posterity. He was a fine draughtsman and his studies of early 19th-century buildings are well worth seeking out.

Heron Pike 2,003ft (610m)
Great Rigg 2,513ft (766m)
Fairfield 2,863ft (873m)
High Pike 2,157ft (657m)
Scar
Erne Crag
Rydale
Low Pike 1,657ft (505m)
Dove Crag 2,603ft (793m)
Queen's Hotel

AMBLESIDE

Queen's Hotel   Salutation Hotel   Market Hall

The Rothay valley was first settled in AD79 by the Romans, who built a fort at Borrans Park beside the lake to protect their supply route over Hardknott and Wrynose Passes to the port of Ravenglass.

Walking and climbing are now a key part of the local economy; not only does the town's plethora of gear shops supply all the necessary equipment, but with fells on three sides and a lake on the other, Ambleside is one of the best places in Lakeland to put it to use.

A walk up 55 stone steps from Lake Road climbs to Lower Gale, from where the town's glorious backdrop of fells can be appreciated without a huge amount of effort.

The untidily placed buildings around Market Place have changed little in appearance over the last century. Victorian trippers used to leave the Queen's Hotel for Ullswater in horse-drawn carriages – which must have made for a terrifying journey over the Kirkstone Pass.

Overlooking Market Place, the Salutation Hotel is one of Ambleside's oldest inns, dating from 1656. It was an important stop on the turnpike road, opened in 1761, where horses were changed for the onward journey to Keswick. A coach would travel between Kendal and Carlisle in about six hours. Ambleside was a focal

Above: **Market Place.**
Below left: **Lake Road.**

AMBLESIDE

point of the Victorian 'cocktail belt', which extended between the town and Grasmere. Alongside the resident Lakeland Poets there was a constant procession of the country's intellectual glitterati – many of whom had second homes in the area.

Harriet Martineau was one incomer who settled in Ambleside, building a house – The Knoll – off Rydal Road in 1845. A formidable woman, now regarded as the first female sociologist, she wrote her *Complete Guide to the English Lakes* in 1855. She argued ferociously with the educated social and literary set – especially Wordsworth, who she considered too right wing. His wife, Mary, used to leave Rydal Mount whenever feisty Martineau called.

The creative glitterati placed Ambleside and its surroundings on the literary tourist map, and in time thousands flocked to the area to walk in the steps of their Romantic heroes. Sadly their influence didn't extend to the local architecture, and Ambleside still hasn't shaken off its air of Victorian grey-slate dullness. Fortunately, the town boasts numerous oddities, including Bridge House, that I'm drawn to – especially if I can draw them too.

Above: The Stamp House – Wordsworth's old (and rarely used) Ambleside office.

The Armitt Library and Museum in Rydal Road is the town's much-acclaimed literary museum containing more than 10,000 items on Lake District history and local personalities. Founded in 1912 by the three Armitt sisters, who devoted themselves to writing and the arts and were supported by the great and good of the time, the museum is a scholarly resource for the local community.

Beatrix Potter donated some of her early watercolour studies of fungi and mosses to the Armitt, demonstrating that artistically she was more than just an illustrator of fluffy bunnies. Far from a dull day out, the museum not only displays a lock of John Ruskin's hair – but with the magic of modern technology you can even talk to him as well!

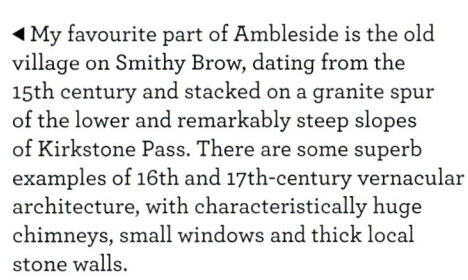

◀ My favourite part of Ambleside is the old village on Smithy Brow, dating from the 15th century and stacked on a granite spur of the lower and remarkably steep slopes of Kirkstone Pass. There are some superb examples of 16th and 17th-century vernacular architecture, with characteristically huge chimneys, small windows and thick local stone walls.

The beck in Stock Ghyll once drove five water mills. One, originally a bark-crushing mill for making tannin used in the leather trade, has been converted to characterful cottages and apartments. Another, an old corn mill, boasts a replica overshot waterwheel.

A lovely walk up Stock Ghyll goes to Stockghyll Force, a spectacular waterfall of some 70ft, plunging in twin ribbons to a rocky basin.

AMBLESIDE

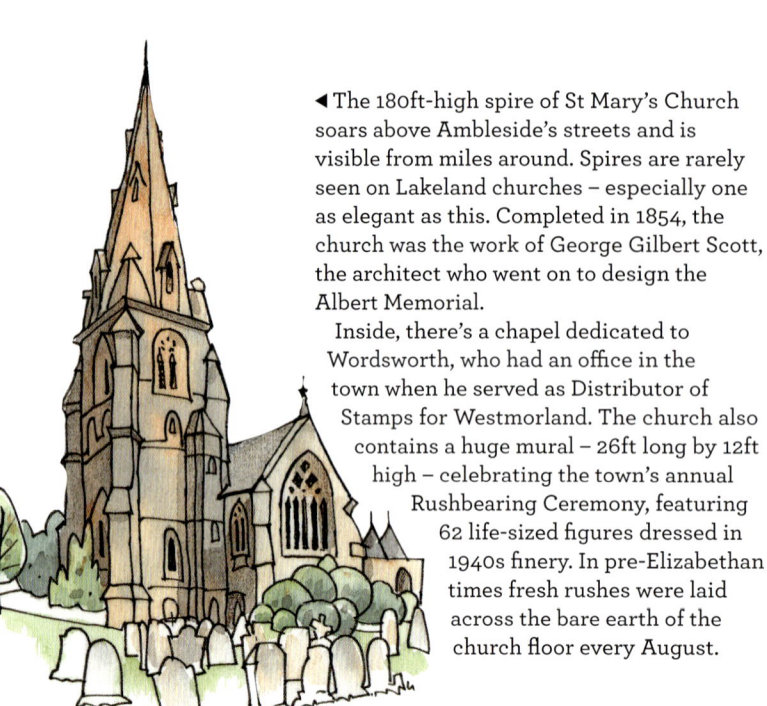

◀ The 180ft-high spire of St Mary's Church soars above Ambleside's streets and is visible from miles around. Spires are rarely seen on Lakeland churches – especially one as elegant as this. Completed in 1854, the church was the work of George Gilbert Scott, the architect who went on to design the Albert Memorial.

Inside, there's a chapel dedicated to Wordsworth, who had an office in the town when he served as Distributor of Stamps for Westmorland. The church also contains a huge mural – 26ft long by 12ft high – celebrating the town's annual Rushbearing Ceremony, featuring 62 life-sized figures dressed in 1940s finery. In pre-Elizabethan times fresh rushes were laid across the bare earth of the church floor every August.

▼ Ash Tree Cottage is typical of the vernacular gems on Smithy Brow – site of the town's first settlement 1,000 years ago. Grade II listed, it dates back to around 1650 with original oak ceiling beams and thick walls.

None of the nearby houses are less than 150 years old and the adjacent How Head Barn boasts a 300-year history, with walls of stone from the Roman fort and oak beams salvaged from ships wrecked off the Cumbrian coast.

AMBLESIDE

▼ Windermere lake ends a mile short of Ambleside at Waterhead – which can come as a surprise to day-trippers who arrive on the ferry from Bowness expecting to set foot in the heart of town. In summer a shuttle-bus runs between the jetty and town centre. A huddle of tourist shops and a couple of pubs do their best to cope with the Waterhead invasion, but day-trippers can also console themselves with the view across the lake, crowded with swans, ducks and boats, all backed by the sublime Langdale Pikes.

Above: **Peggy Hill.**

ELTERWATER

Elter Water

Sitting serenely at the southwestern end of Great Langdale, the riverside village of Elterwater has an industrial history entirely at odds with today's tranquil character. The cluster of cottages, built of green slate from nearby quarries, gather around one of Lakeland's prettiest village greens, with the Britannia Inn at its head and a magnificent maple tree shading a circular wooden seat. It's an idyllic spot, always busy with walkers, cyclists, photographers and Herdwicks.

Elterwater is today almost entirely a tourist village, with only a handful of permanent residents. Most houses are holiday homes.

In days gone by the principal industries of Elterwater were farming, quarrying for slate and gunpowder manufacture. The first two activities continue, while the third – once booming business – is now long gone.

Slate quarrying was well established in the area by the end of the 18th century. In 1824 the quarry owners converted an old bark mill in the village into a gunpowder factory. Locally cut juniper wood was used in the

> " The cluster of cottages, built of green slate from nearby quarries, gather around one of the prettiest village greens in Lakeland.

Little Langdale

Wetherlam
2,502ft (763m)

Swirl How
2,630ft (801m)

Great Carrs
2,575ft (785m)

Elterwater village

Lingmoor Fell
1,530m (466m)

Oakhow Crag

ELTERWATER

manufacturing process. Eighteen waterwheels provided power and up to 90 people were employed. A cannon was fired to test the product.

When demand lessened, the works were closed in 1930, with the buildings demolished and the site redeveloped as a holiday resort. Under new owners in 1981, it was again redeveloped, this time into a luxury time-share with 80 Scandinavian-style lodges built on the 35-acre site and an existing small hotel converted into an exclusive hotel and country club complex.

Right: **Elterwater village green.**
Below: **Elterwater Common on the back road from Grasmere.**

Great Langdale

Crinkle Crags 2,816ft (858m)

Bowfell 2,960ft (902m)

Loft Crag 2,270ft (692m)

Harrison Stickle 2,403ft (732m)

ELTERWATER

Elter Water

At just over half a mile long, with a width that varies hugely with the rainfall and a maximum depth of about 20ft, Elter Water can be a disappointment. Fortunately, the Langdale Pikes are always on hand to make a good background for photos.

Even calling Elter Water a lake may be pushing it a bit, though the three reedy tarns and their soggy surrounds do act as an important holding point for the massive volume of water that flows down the valley from the drainage basin in the dale head fells. Without it the lower valley and Ambleside would suffer even more flooding than they do now.

Above: **Elter Water and the Langdale Pikes.**
Below: **The River Brathay at Skelwith Bridge.**

After rain, Elter Water can double in size, and it has been known to rise as much as five feet in a night. Once a swamp, the lake was deepened by a local developer, John Harden, in 1820 and the low land around it was drained and sold on to local farmers.

An excellent hard-surfaced footpath runs from the village to the lake, then follows the River Brathay to Skelwith Bridge. Skelwith Force on the river is relatively low in height (about 17ft) but water is forced through a narrow rock gap making an impressive fall, especially after rain.

These days, a stroll along the river and a long lunch in Chesters By The River café at Skelwith Bridge is my idea of a day well spent.

ELTERWATER

▶ Like many things nowadays, the village of Elterwater is not what it was. Still attractive and a pleasure to draw, the shop is no more and the Judy Boyes Gallery – one of my favourites – has closed. Any sense of a village community has disappeared with them. We still flock there, but sadly it's for the surroundings rather than the village.

◀ Like Elterwater, Chapel Stile owes its existence to the local slate quarries, some dating back to the 18th century when it was known simply as Langdale Chapel. Holy Trinity Church was built into the fellside in 1857 to replace a chapel of 1750. A contemporary account records that it was in a sorry state of repair, with the pulpit collapsing while the clergyman was reading his sermon. The village is largely untainted by modern developments, though some facilities – a post office and petrol station – have disappeared or changed since I first visited.

▶ On first sight it's easy to think the Wainwrights' Inn at Chapel Stile is yet another Lakeland business cashing in on the great fellwalker's name. Close examination, however, reveals the significant position of the apostrophe after the 's', suggesting the wainwrights referred to are wagon-builders related to the nearby quarries. Or is the name just a canny bit of double-bluff marketing? Either way, the burgers are good.

GREAT LANGDALE

Great Langdale

The valley opens dramatically when you turn the corner and rise out of Chapel Stile, with the majestic Langdale Pikes – some of Lakeland's most iconic fells – beckoning from the head of the valley some three miles distant. The hills lining the lower reaches of the valley lie back like a guard of honour bowing before the star-turns at their head.

The valley forms a lazy 'S' shape, with the occasional house and farm building dotted across its lower hillsides. Most of the time Great Langdale Beck wends an unhurried way through meadows towards Elter Water, but it soon deepens and quickens after heavy rain.

Langdale is big and brash, with all its attractions on show. There are none of the secret nooks and crannies or little sub-valleys you find in Borrowdale. No matter; thousands of visitors are drawn here each year and I'm always happy to be one of them.

Great Langdale is considered to be the oldest inhabited place in the Lake District, with prehistoric rock art found near Chapel Stile, while in 1947 Pike o' Stickle was declared a 5,000-year-old axe factory when Neolithic stone axe-heads were discovered in a gully.

Above: **Dungeon Ghyll.**
Below right: **The Langdale Pikes.**

The Pikes dominate the valley. They're not the highest peaks in the district, but their individual shapes, close grouping and isolation from other fells make them favourites. Generally, there are considered to be three 'Pikes': Pavey Ark, Harrison Stickle and Pike o' Stickle, though Loft Crag and Thorn Crag are sometimes added.

Crinkle Crags 2,816ft (858m)
Old Dungeon Ghyll Ho
Oxendale
The Band
Mickleden

GREAT LANGDALE

The fabulous amphitheatre of mountains arrayed across the head of the valley also vie for attention. Here, Great Langdale divides in two: Oxendale heads southwest, initially tracked by a narrow road that climbs into Little Langdale; while Mickleden, a busy highway for walkers taking the Stake Pass route into Borrowdale, strikes northwest.

I stayed overnight at the New Dungeon Ghyll Hotel on my Cumbria Way journey. Starting a walk immediately after breakfast was a privilege new to me. In bright sunshine I strode out across the fellside beneath Raven Crag and Middlefell Buttress – great slabs of rock much loved by generations of climbers.

> **"** Starting a walk immediately after breakfast was a privilege new to me.

In Mickleden I was intrigued by the series of moraines, left by melting glaciers, which look like enormous molehills scattered across the valley floor. Shortly after passing the glacial hummocks, the path rises to ascend Stake Pass, an exhilarating climb with fine views of Bow Fell and Crinkle Crags before the summit of the pass arrives at an altitude close to that of its nearest Pike, Pike o' Stickle.

As I surveyed the scene from the pass, I was in for a surprise: the area around the back of the mighty Pikes is not only grassy but relatively flat. All the craggy, exciting bits are on display at the front, facing the valley. Nature – the great window dresser.

Bow Fell 2,960ft (902m)
Middlefell Buttress
Pike o' Stickle 2,323ft (708m)
Raven Crag
Dungeon Ghyll
Loft Crag 2,238ft (682m)
Thorn Crag 2,200ft (671m)
Harrison Stickle 2,403ft (732m)
New Dungeon Ghyll Hotel
Stickle Tarn
Pavey Ark 2,288ft (697m)

DUNGEON GHYLL

Langdale is blessedly untouched by modern development; even the road is narrow and twisting, and the main facilities at Dungeon Ghyll have a delightfully old-fashioned charm about them. There are two hotels: the 'Old' (over 300 years old) and the 'New' Dungeon Ghyll Hotel (built 1862).

The National Trust's popular campsite at Dungeon Ghyll, on the other hand, is state-of-the-art, boasting pods, yurts and Nordic tipis, and a shop selling baked bread. It even has its own pub, the excellent Sticklebarn Tavern.

The traditional clientele of the Old Dungeon Ghyll Hotel at the valley head might once have scoffed at luxury. In its early years, rock climbing pioneers would gather here for riotous weeks of drinking, partying and scaling the surrounding crags. These days the hotel has well-manicured en-suite rooms and – *gasp!* – four-poster beds.

Above: **Pavey Ark.**
Below: **Stickle Ghyll.**
Below right: **The Old Dungeon Ghyll.**

A popular walk from Dungeon Ghyll is the steep climb up Stickle Ghyll to Stickle Tarn, dammed in 1838 to maintain a head of water for the Elterwater Gunpowder Factory. The well-trodden path follows a tumbling beck, interrupted at two-thirds height by a cascade that after wet weather can be spectacular.

Feeding the Ghyll, Stickle Tarn is set in a scene of rocky splendour. The cliff bastion of Pavey Ark looms over it, darkening the still waters of the tarn with its sombre reflection.

Jack's Rake, a curious slanting terrace, crosses Pavey Ark, running diagonally from bottom right to top left. It's a popular challenge for adventurous fell walkers, but a dangerous place for anyone else. Even Wainwright couldn't face it for many years.

BLEA TARN

In *The Excursion* Wordsworth portrayed Blea Tarn as "A liquid pool that glittered in the sun, and one bare dwelling; one abode, no more!", a description which still applies today.

Harriet Martineau described the connection between the Great and Little Langdale valleys as "a very rough road". She was referring to its suitability for horses, but, again, the description remains apt. Wordsworth's "one bare dwelling" is Blea Tarn House, beautifully situated and now part private dwelling, part climber's bothy.

The tarn, backed by woods

Above: **Blea Tarn and the Langdale Pikes.**
Below: **Blea Tarn House.**

and crags and nestled in an upland valley, is a Lakeland icon as picturesque as anyone could wish for. I've drawn and painted the scene a few times but have never quite captured the magic of the wind around my ears and the visual feast in whichever direction you choose to face.

The introduced pine plantations around the tarn make the scene look less desolate than it once did; a reminder that these valleys – like most of Lakeland – were once forested up to the 2,000ft contour, when the higher fells must have looked like rocky islands in a sea of vegetation.

LITTLE LANGDALE

Above: **Slater's Bridge.**
Below: **Cottages in Little Langdale.**

Little Langdale

After the dramatics of the lion next door, Little Langdale is a pussy cat; a restful gem of a valley set in a half-hidden green hollow featuring a scattering of buildings and backed by the Coniston fells.

Only accessible by narrow lanes, Little Langdale is protected in the west by the steep mountain pass to Wrynose, while to the east thick woodland screens the valley from a busy world. The twisty approaches carry off-putting signs warning of the twin perils motorists face from the Wrynose and Hardknott Passes ahead.

Little Langdale Tarn, the main source of the River Brathay, lies to the west, resembling a large flood in a field and lacking any scenic qualities at all. By contrast, immediately after the outflow, Slater's Bridge is the most picturesque footbridge in Lakeland, a slender slate arch built by miners to give them a short-cut to work in the Tilberthwaite quarries. It always reminds me of an illustration in a children's fairytale book.

LITTLE LANGDALE

Little Langdale's isolation was the attraction for Lanty Slee, a farmer, quarryman and – most famously – notorious smuggler.

Slee was born in Borrowdale around 1800 and operated multiple illicit stills making moonshine whisky in Little Langdale. He even ran a profitable exporting business using packhorses to smuggle his product over Wrynose and Hardknott Passes to Ravenglass. On the return journey the ponies brought back tobacco.

In 1840 Slee built Greenbank Farm in Little Langdale, where he lived before moving to Low Arnside. He died at the age of 78, mourned by his many clients – some even rumoured to be peers of the realm. The locations of his many stills in the valley died with him, but are still sought out by admirers.

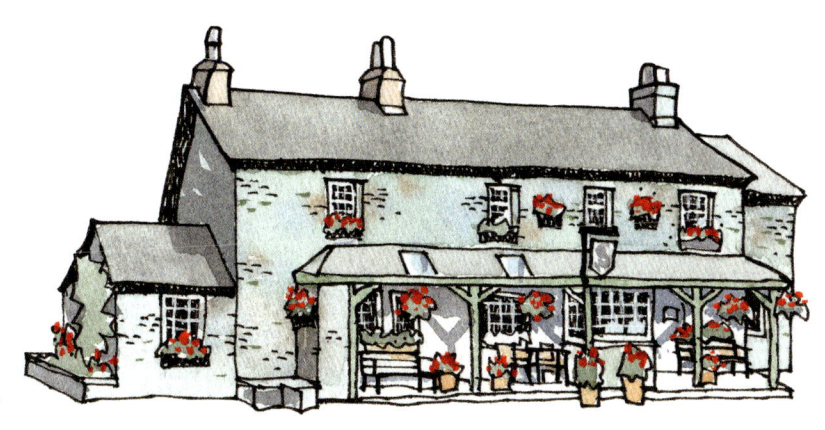

Above: **The Three Shires Inn.**
Below: **Fell Foot Farm.**

▲ The name of the Three Shires Inn in Little Langdale refers to the meeting point of the old counties of Cumberland, Westmorland and Lancashire high on Wrynose Pass.

▼ Fell Foot Farm stands at the foot of the pass. The road twists around it before starting its climb. It is rumoured the farm was once part of Lanty Slee's operations.

Windermere & Bowness

Trains, boats, follies and vernacular gems

As befits England's largest lake, Windermere has a stately air and is named after a Norse hero, Vinandr. The lake is ten and a half miles long and a mile wide in places, with a maximum depth of 219ft. Belle Isle, the largest of Windermere's 18 islands, almost cuts the lake in two at Bowness. In ancient times the lake was a busy Roman highway, later used to transport iron ore and charcoal. These days all manner of boats scrum for a stretch of clear water. Large powerboats were banned from the lake when a 10mph speed limit became effective in 2005.

Most of the shoreline is thickly wooded, and the lake's east side has long been a magnet for visitors. At the end of the 18th century this stretch became a fashionable haunt of wealthy mill owners from Manchester and Liverpool, who set about changing the place to suit their ideas of Arcadia. Flashy villas and fanciful temples sprang up along the lakeshore and exotic woodland was planted to screen them from the masses. Many of these mansions still stand – now as luxury hotels.

The quieter west side of the lake is very different, with a narrow road running as far as Sawrey and a genial lakeside path.

Left: **Windermere shops.**
Right: **MV Teal** about to dock at Lakeside.

WINDERMERE & BOWNESS

◀ Brockhole House was built at the end of the 19th century as the holiday home of wealthy silk merchant William Gaddum and his wife Edith (née) Potter – cousin to Beatrix Potter. It is now acclaimed as one of the lesser-known Arts & Crafts treasures of Cumbria. The Lake District National Park Authority purchased the house and grounds in 1966, opening it in 1969 as the UK's first National Park Visitor Centre. Restoration and redevelopment has turned it into today's multi-activity centre.

Windermere town

Most English towns begin life with a market charter. Windermere started with a railway station. This opened in 1848 when the line arrived at the hamlet of Birthwaite, which rapidly developed into a holiday town and eventually adopted the station name of Windermere.

A local company, Pattinsons, built the station and at the same time constructed the splendid Windermere Hotel opposite, which overlooks the station and town.

Plans to extend the line to Grasmere were abandoned following opposition led by Ruskin, Rawnsley and Wordsworth; what a tourist draw that line would have been today – possibly taking a few cars off the A591 at the same time.

By the 1960s the number of visitors arriving by train had fallen, and in 1976 one line was taken up, leaving only a single track to Oxenholme. The original station was abandoned in 1983 and a year later a Booths supermarket opened on the site, retaining the striking entrance that once led to the station booking office.

A new station was opened in 1985, costing £90,000 and paid for by a joint British Rail and local action group effort. It's built of wood and hung with baskets of flowers in classic 'country twee' style.

Windermere traffic is legendary, not helped by the layout of the town. Crescent Road and Main Street form a banana shape enclosing a tight collection of Gothic Victorian buildings, many now with modern shop fronts. Both are one-way streets.

A desperate measure to reduce summer traffic volume through the town was experimented with in 1990, when all road signs to Bowness were covered for three months. The lakeside businesses were not pleased and, unsurprisingly, the experiment has never been repeated.

Acme House, one of the town's most historic buildings, thrusts like a wedge between the northern junction of Crescent Road and Main Street. Once the Embassy Cinema, the building now houses Brown Sugar, a contemporary restaurant, bar and meeting place.

Above: **Brown Sugar.**
Below: **Windermere station.**

WINDERMERE TOWN

The old-school Queen's Hotel across the road has a beer garden perilously close to the traffic, which enables its lively clientele to jeer at sweating motorists crawling past.

Despite drifting towards becoming a totally tourist town, Windermere still hangs on to some 'proper' shops amidst the plethora of bars, restaurants, coffee shops, souvenir emporiums and takeaways. There's a large hardware shop in Main Street and a family butchers in Crescent Road. You can still buy a sofa or a book, have your eyes tested and make an appointment to have a tooth extracted. Best of all, most businesses remain owned and run by local people.

I'm from the other side of Dunmail Raise, so Windermere always feels foreign to me. Parking in the town is a particular bugbear.

Booths' large car park is strictly for shoppers, and the only other official parking involves driving blindly around a series of enclaves off Broad Street hoping – often in vain – to find a space.

Above: **Crescent Street in 1990.**
Below: **Queen's Hotel.**

ORREST HEAD

A lane across the road from the station climbs to the popular viewpoint of Orrest Head, an easy 20-minute stroll.

"Here the promised land is seen in all its glory," wrote Alfred Wainwright, after he first saw the view while on holiday at the age of 23. Since then many more people, inspired by his example, have stood here and vowed to climb all 214 of the designated 'Wainwright summits'. Sadly, considering its importance in triggering Wainwright's fell-bagging odyssey, Orrest Head has a summit rising only to around 783ft; it's not even listed amongst his revered 214. It does, however, appear in AW's *Outlying Fells of Lakeland*, where he suggests a round trip, up and down from Windermere train station.

Above: The lane to Orrest Head.
Below: View north from Orrest Head.

The view from the unremarkable nobble of rock that forms the summit is impressive, though for those of us lucky enough to have been raised amongst the fells, it's hardly life-changing. But to a young visitor from the smoke and grime of 1930s Blackburn, the effect was understandably profound.

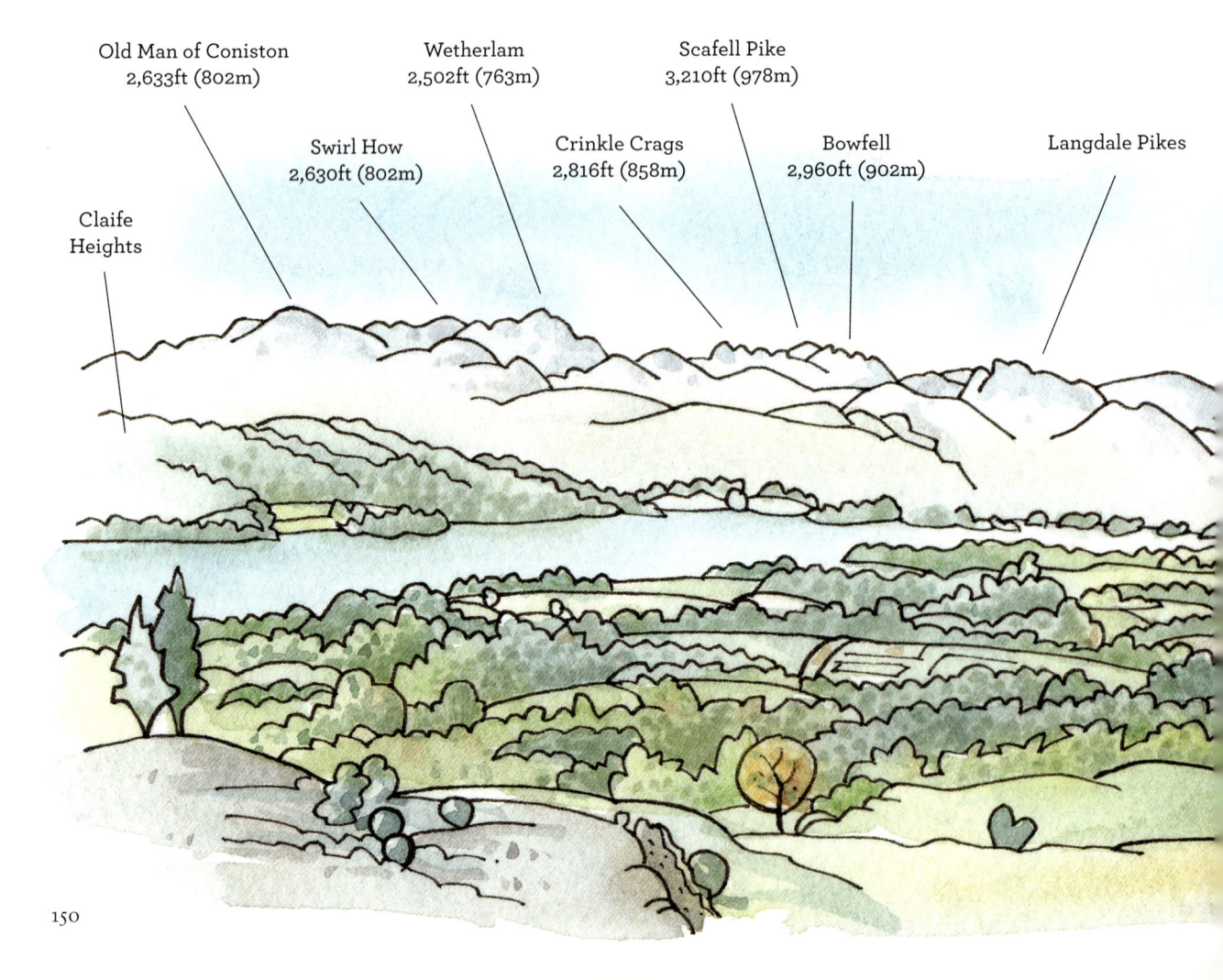

Claife Heights

Old Man of Coniston
2,633ft (802m)

Swirl How
2,630ft (802m)

Wetherlam
2,502ft (763m)

Crinkle Crags
2,816ft (858m)

Scafell Pike
3,210ft (978m)

Bowfell
2,960ft (902m)

Langdale Pikes

ORREST HEAD

▶ Blackburn-born Alfred Wainwright left school at the age of 13, before years of evening study led him to qualify as a municipal accountant. He was inspired by the view from Orrest Head when he first saw it in 1930 and yearned to live near the fells. Eventually, he moved his family to Kendal in 1941, where he became Borough Treasurer.

His classic seven volumes of *Pictorial Guides* were completed between 1955 and 1966 – all written and drawn in his own hand. He went on to write and illustrate over 40 books, mostly about Lakeland. Sales from his books have been estimated at over £4 million.

I have a tenuous link to AW. In his guide to the northern fells he refers to "curious looped tracks on the fellside" in the ascent of Blencathra via Roughton Gill being "the result of motor-bike scrambling by the village lads". I was one of those lads. Not – I hasten to add – driving a bike, but clinging to the back of one of my pals who was doing the difficult stuff.

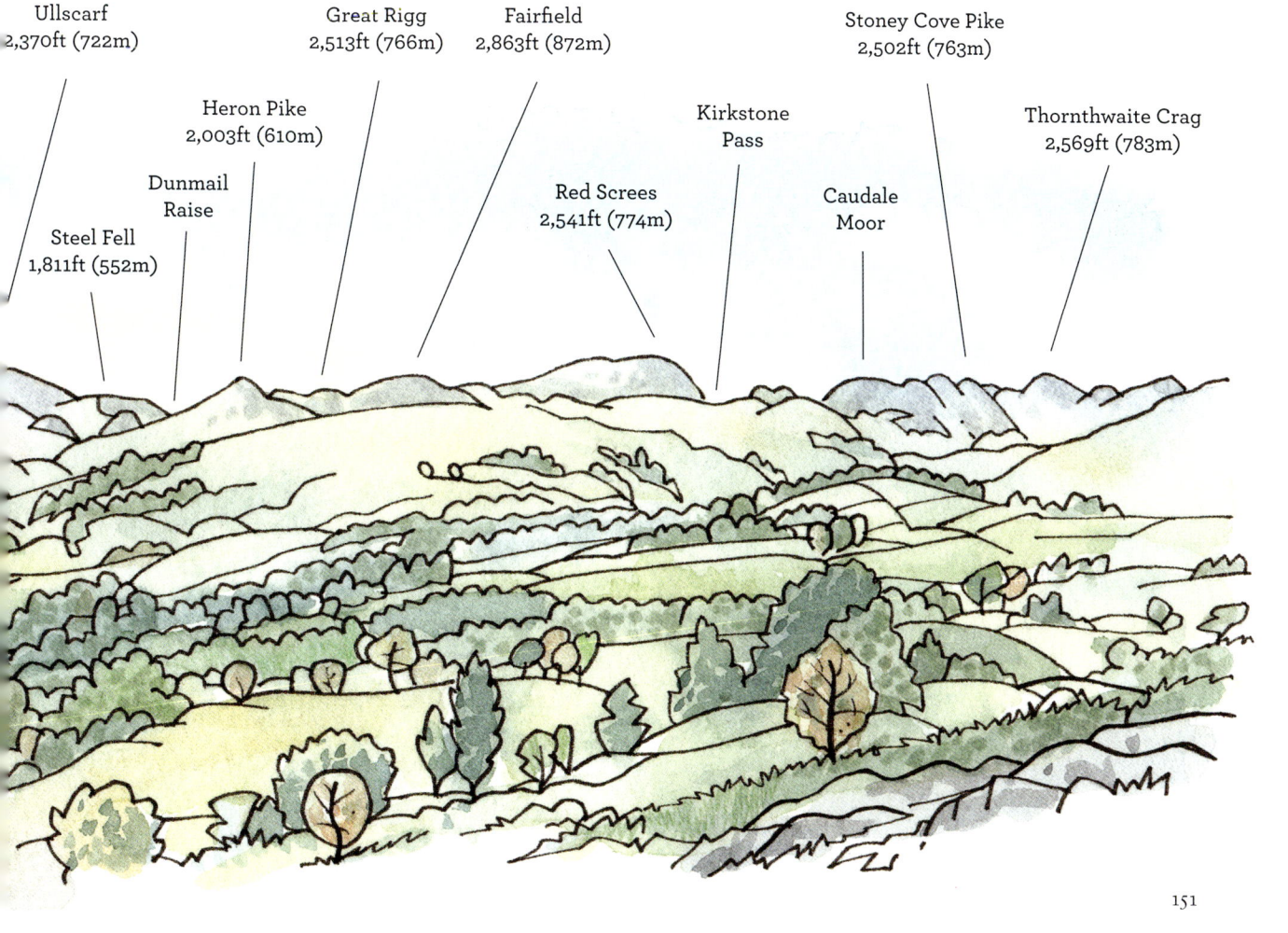

Ullscarf 2,370ft (722m)
Great Rigg 2,513ft (766m)
Fairfield 2,863ft (872m)
Stoney Cove Pike 2,502ft (763m)
Heron Pike 2,003ft (610m)
Kirkstone Pass
Thornthwaite Crag 2,569ft (783m)
Dunmail Raise
Red Screes 2,541ft (774m)
Caudale Moor
Steel Fell 1,811ft (552m)

BOWNESS

Bowness

The ancient village of Bowness is now irrevocably attached to the railway town of Windermere, and together they make up the biggest settlement in the Lake District National Park, with a population of some 11,000. On a sunny bank holiday there's probably another 11,000 visitors crammed into the narrow streets.

The rest of the time Bowness is merely *busy* – typically with coachloads of older folk and foreign tourists anxious to sample the English Lake District.

What they experience is not typical of Lakeland. And while the row of shops climbing Crag Brow has a certain… something, it's certainly not taste or elegance.

One of Bowness' best features, a magnificent chestnut tree at the foot of Crag Brow, was shamefully cut down under the cover of darkness in 2018 for 'health and safety' reasons. The tree was the last remaining of three planted in 1900.

Amongst the cavalcade of drab Victoriana, gift shops and takeaway food outlets, the peaceful Church of St Martin, set amongst ancient yew trees (uncut!), is a blessed relief.

A church has stood on this site since 1203, although the present building dates from 1436. Medieval glass from Cartmel Priory was brought here for safety during the Dissolution and incorporated into the east window; it is St Martin's greatest treasure. The churchyard was consecrated during the Great Plague of 1348 and some of the yew trees are well over 600 years old.

My favourite part of Bowness is the old road behind the church, where there are attractive scenes to draw

Top: Crag Brow – before the chestnut tree in Queen's Square was axed.
Above: A restaurant doorway.
Below: St Martin's Church.

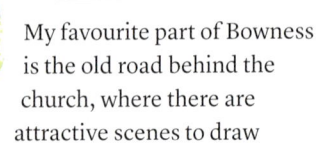

BOWNESS

and a few historic curiosities. I like to sketch doorways, and I'm always gratified by the effort people put into making the entrances to their businesses attractive and inviting. In that respect, Bowness can be relied upon to put on a good show.

The 17th-century New Hall Inn is locally know as 'Hole in t' Wall', from the time when sweaty blacksmiths in the smithy next door were passed tankards of ale through a... hole in the wall.

A sign outside stretches facts by boasting it was 'frequented by Charles Dickens'. Another states that from 1852 to 1860 the landlord was Thomas Longmire, 'champion wrestler of England and holder of 174 titles'. What the sign doesn't say is that his wrestling prowess was in the local Cumberland and Westmorland style of combat... Though I wouldn't argue the point with Mr Longmire if he was still around.

Above: **Churchills Tavern and The White House bar, in Robinson Place.**
Below: **Hole in t' Wall pub.**

Sawpit Hill is nearby. Most parts of rural England used to have such a pit, where one woodman stood below the log and another above to heave the long saw. Sounds like thirsty work, wherever you stood. Luckily Hole in t' Wall wasn't far away.

WINDERMERE

Windermere lake

Despite my ungraciousness towards Bowness, the gloom usually lifts when I walk onto the promenade and the view across the lake to Belle Isle opens up. It's best when crowded, when the sun is shining, big white boats are being loaded and geese and swans wander for scraps. It's a scene that needs people and energy. When only a few folk are about, it's not the same.

The promenade is overlooked by the Belsfield Hotel, home of H. W. Schneider in the late 19th century. He used to commute each day to his office in Barrow, eating breakfast while travelling by launch down the lake to Lakeside then by private carriage on the Furness Railway to Barrow. His schedule was reversed in the evening, getting home in time for dinner.

Ah, those were the days… Especially when you owned the house, pier, launch, railway and ironworks company.

There has been a ferry service across Windermere for at least 500 years. Originally large rowing boats – often dangerously overcrowded – made the trip. In 1635, a ferry carrying 47 people and 11 horses sank with no survivors.

The first cable ferry, powered by steam, started operating in 1870, pulling itself along on two cables strung across the lake bed.

The present ferry, named Mallard, was built in 1990 on the Welsh coast and carries up to 18 vehicles and 100 pedestrians. The four-minute crossing cuts out a road journey to Sawrey of around 14 miles.

As the only static ferry across any of the lakes, it has become a tourist attraction itself.

Above: **Old England Hotel and the waterfront.**
Below left: **An early ferry.**

▼ Belle Isle, the largest island on Windermere, covers 37 acres and is the only one that is privately owned and inhabited. Peeping through the trees, Belle Isle House was built in 1774, the first neoclassical calendar house in England. It is reputed to be the country's only truly round house. Originally the house had 365 panes of glass, 52 windows, 12 rooms and four sculptures – which qualified it for the 'calendar' tag. Following a devastating fire in 1996, the house has been restored and reinhabited but, together with the island, it is strictly private.

WINDERMERE

▼ Windermere Lake Cruises operate a fleet of 17 vessels that sail every day of the year bar Christmas Day. Two of the four largest 'steamers' can carry over 500 passengers and the oldest, Swan, was built at Barrow in 1938. The latest, Swift, was launched in 2020, built in the Netherlands, shipped in sections and assembled at the Windermere lakeside. I like to walk on past the boatyards to Cockshott Point, site of a seaplane factory and pilot training facility during the First World War. The factory closed in the 1920s and it's now a popular picnic spot with fine views along the lake.

Above: The wonderful Victorian designs of the pier entrances on the promenade are a delight.
Right: Swan.

WINDERMERE

South of Bowness, Windermere loses interest in being England's largest lake and gradually dwindles in width to become the River Leven at Newby Bridge.

Crossing the bridge onto the west side of the lake is quite a transformation. The busy eastern shore is almost all privately owned, but here the heavily wooded shore is more tranquil and you can get close to the water.

At Lakeside an absence of trees reveals open views of the lake. Lakeside is also home to the Lakeside and Haverthwaite Steam Railway and Lakes Aquarium.

The railway is the sole surviving part of a line that once stretched to Ulverston and Barrow. After closing in 1965, part of it was reopened as a heritage line in 1973. Steam locos now puff along four miles of wooded track beside the River Leven.

Nearby Stott Park Bobbin Mill was founded in 1835 to supply the nearby textile industry with wooden bobbins. At one time 250 men and boys were employed. With the decline of the cotton industry and the introduction of plastic bobbins, commercial production ended in 1971, but the mill lives on as a visitor attraction. Bobbin making was once a vibrant Lakeland industry, with fast-flowing rivers driving the mills and a ready supply of coppiced wood from nearby hillsides.

Claife Station is an 18th-century curiosity near the ferry house built as a 'banqueting house' by John Curwen, who lived in Island House on Belle Isle. Curwen was an MP, cultural reformer and leading light of the period. One of his great gifts was the planting of 800,000 deciduous trees along the west shore of Windermere. Dances and parties were held in his banqueting house, which included a wine cellar and kitchen. Each window in the house had different-coloured glass to suggest the four seasons.

Above: **Newby Bridge.**
Bottom left: **Stott Park Bobbin Mill.**
Bottom right: **Claife Station.**

WINDERMERE

▼ Wray Castle at Low Wray is not a real castle, but certainly my idea of what a proper one should look like. The edifice was built during the 1840s by Dr James Dawson, a Liverpool surgeon, using his wife's inheritance from a gin fortune as finance. With seemingly unlimited resources, he really went for it, ordering a portcullis, turrets, as well as arrow slits – even mock ruins in the grounds. What started as a retirement house for him and his wife became an expansive Gothic fantasy. Sadly, Mrs Dawson took one look at the finished house and refused to live in it.

I love it – not to live in, of course – but the castle is wonderful to draw while dreaming of being a medieval nobleman and master of the Windermere lakeshore.

Over the years the castle has had many uses – even as a holiday home for a young Beatrix Potter. Now owned by the National Trust, the castle, gardens and walks down to the lake are open as a family-friendly attraction.

Right: 'Where's the Castle?': Walkers at Low Wray.
Below: Wray Castle.

TROUTBECK

Troutbeck

A three-and-a-half-mile green valley thrusts northwards from Windermere, with the settlement of Troutbeck basking seductively on its western slopes. The main A592 road to Ullswater takes a lower route, leaving the village in peace for walkers and lovers of vernacular architecture, for whom Troutbeck is endlessly fascinating.

Almost every building in the Troutbeck valley is over 300 years old. The surrounding mountain landscape is magnificent, rising to over 2,500ft at the head of the valley. Trout Beck itself rises amongst its slopes and meanders blissfully through woods and farmland before plunging through steep ravines into Windermere.

Beatrix Potter was so enamoured with this valley she bought Troutbeck Park Farm, a run-down 1,900-acre sheep farm at its head, in 1923. With Tom Storey, her faithful shepherd, she built up a celebrated flock of Herdwick sheep and continued her emerging mission to save Lakeland farm estates from eager-eyed (and deep-pocketed) industrialist developers.

She considered Troutbeck valley her favourite place. It's easy to see why; her muse is all around.

▲ Troutbeck Village Shop and Tea Room, built on the hillside around 1870, is distinctive enough to be considered the village centre. Entrance to the public hall is from further up the hillside in traditional bank barn-fashion. The Old Post Office Tearoom on the ground floor sells essentials plus drinks and freshly cooked food. Their Kendal-made flapjacks are the best. A Post Office counter is open two days a week.

Above: Townhead, as seen on numerous postcards, calendars and magazine covers.

TROUTBECK

▼ Troutbeck consists of a series of houses and farms strung out over a mile of narrow road. Ancient lanes criss-cross and connect the clusters of buildings gathered around roadside wells. Many houses are slate-built using stone from the valley's 18th-century quarries.

A cluster of fine houses and bank barns at the north end, High Green, makes a wonderful composition, the white-rendered houses contrasting with dark slate. A carefully preserved spinning gallery is hidden amongst the buildings – a reminder of Troutbeck's sheep farming heritage.

Clock Cottage is nearby, with a clock mounted on the gale end. The last time I was here, it had stopped at a quarter to 11. Time really does stand still in Troutbeck...

> " The last time I was here, the clock had stopped at a quarter to 11. Time really does stand still in Troutbeck...

Right: Spinning gallery.

TROUTBECK

◀ Originally the site of a 17th-century inn, Mortal Man is a large, rambling building largely rebuilt when tourists started flocking to Troutbeck in the 19th century. The inn sign carries a peculiar rhyme:

O mortal man, that lives by bread,
What is it that makes thy nose so red?
Thou silly fool, that looks't so pale,
'Tis drinking Sally Birkett's ale.

Possibly Sally Birkett was an early landlady of the Mortal Man, but nobody seems to know. Apart from its famous sign, the inn also has a perennially popular beer garden with sensational views over the valley.

▶ High Fold Farmhouse stands at the entrance to a small courtyard where 17th and 19th-century houses compete with modern barn and granary conversions as holiday accommodation. According to the village website, approximately 40% of Troutbeck houses are second homes or holiday lets.

◀ 'Jaunie Wife House' is the curious name for a white-fronted dwelling that appears to be split into two abodes. Stone-slabbed steps still lead to what used to be the first-floor granary, while a barn cut into the hillside has been converted to a garage. Hanging baskets and pink hydrangeas complete the picture of a quintessential rural idyll.

TROUTBECK

▲ Of all the historic houses in Troutbeck, the finest is undoubtedly Townend.

George Browne, a wealthy yeoman sheep farmer, whose family were well-established in the village, built the substantial house in 1626 on the site of an earlier building. It remained in the Browne family until it was gifted to the National Trust in 1947.

Throughout the house, intricately carved furniture and quirky domestic tools provide a window into the lives and personalities of generations of Brownes. The library contains the family's well-thumbed collection of books, including 45 that are the only remaining copies in the world.

A large bank barn across the road is where the Brownes stored wool fleeces until they were sold on to merchants. Located on a hillside, Troutbeck has dozens of bank barns. They are noted for entrances on two separate levels, one higher up the hillside – where hay was stored – and the second below.

Top: Townend.
Above: The Brownes' bank barn.
Left: Layout of a typical bank barn.

Hawkshead & Coniston

Potter, Wordsworth, Ruskin and Ransome

Pike o' Blisco
2,304ft (702m)

Bowfell
2,960ft (902m)

Rossett Pike
2,106ft (642m)

Pike o' Stickle
2,403ft (732m)

Loft Crag
2,238ft (682m)

Harrison Stickle
2,415ft (736m)

Pavey Ark
2,288ft (697m)

High Raise
2,500ft (762m)

Sergeant Man
2,414ft (736m)

Steel Fell
1,811ft (552m)

TARN HOWS

Coach tour operators market the area between Windermere and Coniston as 'Beatrix Potter Country'. As marketing strategies go the description is fairly accurate, as at one time the author and farmer owned a great deal of it. Not only that, but the landscape itself has a familiar air of Potterism about it, with whitewashed cottages, low rolling hills, woodland and quiet stretches of water. Many local scenes feature in her books.

The area's main landscape draw, Tarn Hows, is pure Potter and not your usual Lakeland tarn. This one has car parks, toilets and over a million visitors a year. The half-mile-long tarn, set in a bowl of low, lushly wooded hills, has islands, peninsulas and a panoramic background of fells – surprisingly extensive from such a low vantage point. Like a romantic stage set, the scene is so perfect it looks unreal; which in some ways it is. Tarn Hows is a man-made landscape feature that first appeared in about 1914, when the landowners, the Marshall family, built a dam, converting a number of small tarns into a larger one with two small islands. Beatrix Potter bought Tarn Hows in 1929 as part of the 4,000-acre Monk Coniston estate, which was later bequeathed to the National Trust.

Extensive landscaping, hard footpaths, and footbridges make it more artificial every year. Nevertheless, despite its detractors and occasional overcrowding, Tarn Hows on a bright, clear morning is a scene of unforgettable beauty.

That's how I saw it on my Cumbria Way walk from Coniston. I've never seen it look so perfect before or since; a fleeting moment I'll never forget.

Above: **High Yewdale Farm. One of the 15 farms that Beatrix Potter left to the National Trust.**
Below: **Tarn Hows.**

Tom Heights 882ft (269m)
Helvellyn 3,118ft (950m)
Seat Sandal 2,415ft (736m)
Fairfield 2,863ft (874m)
Hart Crag 2,698ft (822m)
Dove Crag 2,603ft (793m)
Black Fell 1,056ft (322m)
Red Screes 2,541ft (774m)

NEAR SAWREY

Old Man of Coniston
2,633ft (802m)

Wetherlam
2,502ft (763m)

Crinkle Crags
2,816ft (858m)

Pike o' Blisco
2,304ft (702m)

Bowfell
2,960ft (902m)

Above: Near Sawrey from the Windermere road.

Near Sawrey

Despite the worldwide fame of Beatrix Potter, its most celebrated resident, and the flood of thousands that visit her Hill Top house weekly, the hamlet of Near Sawrey retains its dignity and remains the most decorous and unflashy of all Lakeland honeypots.

The cluster of white-painted traditional cottages nestle in a shallow vale, with meadows spreading down the hillside to the quiet lake of Esthwaite Water. Low hills are dotted with woodland, dry-stone walls line meadows where rabbits play. It all seems so familiar – so perfect – just as it is in the Potter books. When I visit, I half expect to meet a duck wearing a mop cap.

▼ The National Trust is passionate about preserving Hill Top from tourist damage. Visitor numbers are controlled, coaches banned and there is little nearby in the way of car parking. It must be one of the few Trust houses where visitors are actually *discouraged* – but all in a good cause.

NEAR SAWREY

> **Potter's love of Lakeland was profound and she contributed much to its conservation and traditions.**

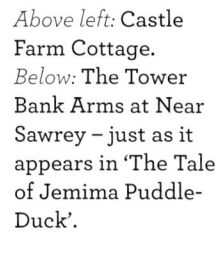

Following her purchase of Hill Top, Beatrix Potter had an extension built for her farm manager, while she remained in London caring for her parents. She visited when she could and did some of her best work in the hillside cottage.

After marrying, Beatrix and husband William Heelis lived in nearby Castle Farm Cottage – though she kept ownership of Hill Top as a workplace and a museum to Lakeland farming life.

Country life developed in her a strong belief in the preservation of rural Lakeland, a conviction she shared with Canon Rawnsley, co-founder of the National Trust.

Energised by developers buying Lakeland farms as second homes, she bought several estates over the years, believing that they should be kept together as working farm units. They were all left to the Trust in her will, along with Hill Top.

Above left: Castle Farm Cottage.
Below: The Tower Bank Arms at Near Sawrey – just as it appears in 'The Tale of Jemima Puddle-Duck'.

Beatrix Potter (1865–1943)

Born in London to genteel, upper-middle-class Victorian parents, Beatrix Potter was educated at home, but found artistic outlet – in her words – "drawing and painting little books for children".

Family holidays were spent in grand, rented houses in the Lake District, where a family friend, Canon Rawnsley, encouraged her to self-publish. Her first book, *The Tale of Peter Rabbit*, was published in 1901 with a limited print run.

A year later it was republished by Messrs Warne, who went on to handle all later titles. With the money she made from her palm-sized books, she bought Hill Top Farm at Near Sawrey in 1905.

At the age of 47, Beatrix Potter married William Heelis, a local solicitor, and devoted the rest of her life to the preservation of farms and the countryside, becoming a respected expert on, and breeder of, Herdwick sheep.

When she died in 1943, all of her property – 15 farms with hefted flocks, a string of cottages and 4,000 acres of land – was left to the National Trust.

I've a soft spot for Beatrix Potter. Not for her books, which, despite the superb illustrations, I find a bit twee (though they do have dark undertones). Instead I admire the fact that, despite the societal expectations on an upper-middle-class woman, she ploughed her own furrow. Her love of Lakeland was profound and she contributed much to its conservation and traditions. Most of all, in later life she looked just like my granny.

ESTHWAITE WATER

Wetherlam 2,502ft (763m)
Crinkle Crags 2,816ft (858m)
Bowfell 2,960ft (902m)
Langdale Pikes
Tarn Hows

Esthwaite Water

Only a modest one and a half miles long, around 700 yards wide and barely 80ft deep, Esthwaite Water is one of the smallest and least visited of the region's lakes. Surrounded by low fells, woodland and minor roads, Esthwaite Water is appealingly pretty, with a great view of the Langdale Pikes from the Hawkshead to Windermere road.

Esthwaite Water is to Hawkshead what Coniston Water is to Coniston and Derwent Water is to Keswick. Which is to say, the settlement is not at the lakeside, and there's a half-mile footpath from Hawkshead to the lake.

Above: Esthwaite Water from the Hawkshead to Windermere road.

Car park access is near a trout fishery on the far southern shore. Trout, perch and roach can all be found in the lake.

As a schoolboy, William Wordsworth lodged with Mrs Tyson at Colthouse, a few fields from the lake. He knew Esthwaite Water well and mentions skating on it fondly in his semi-autobiographical magnum opus, *The Prelude*.

Ospreys nest at Esthwaite Water, but, unlike those at Bassenthwaite, they are allowed to breed away from the glare of publicity; apart from their remarkable flying and fishing abilities, the Esthwaite birds also show impressive good sense.

Hawkshead

Hawkshead

With the character of a small market town rather than a village, Hawkshead's compact and unco-ordinated arrangement of ancient whitewashed buildings, cobbled pavements, narrow streets and low archways leading to secluded courtyards is a joy to explore. Hawkshead is unlike any other village – or town – in the Lake District. It also has connections with both William Wordsworth and Beatrix Potter.

The area was part of Furness Abbey during the 12th century – once the most powerful Cistercian monastery in the country.

Coniston was too far away for the parent abbey near Barrow-in-Furness to manage, so the monks established a 'grange' at Hawkshead. This became an important business centre dealing with the wood, iron and wool trades. Wool was particularly important; Hawkshead supplied most of the wool that was exported to Europe.

After the dissolution of the monasteries in 1536–41, a yeoman class of farmers and landowners began to develop, becoming some of Lakeland's most powerful families.

The town hall was built in 1790 and the five open-arched shops at square level were occupied on market days by butchers. Hawkshead boasts 68 listed buildings including the classic red phone box outside the town hall designed by Giles Gilbert Scott.

Above: **Main Street.**
Below: **Hawkshead Town Hall.**

Road traffic, banned from the village, is directed into a big car park on its outskirts. You have to negotiate a street of retail outlets before entering the hallowed cobbles of the village proper.

We used to play cricket at Hawkshead and our team bus had to negotiate the narrow and twisting main street before the big car park was built.

The bus driver always had his stock one-liner ready: "Right, everybody breathe in." Hilarious – though the corners of various buildings along Main Street carry the scars of vehicles failing to breathe in as they drove through the village.

HAWKSHEAD

The Beatrix Potter Gallery, a 17th-century building in Main Street, was once the office of local solicitor William Heelis, who married Beatrix Potter in 1913. The Heelis law firm had been in the village since 1861 and William was a partner from 1900 until his death in 1945, when the building passed to the National Trust.

His office is preserved and the remainder of the gallery is devoted to his wife, with an annually changing exhibition featuring a selection of her drawings and illustrations.

The National Trust also owns many other buildings in the village – which almost helps to preserve Hawkshead as a museum piece itself.

Above, top: **King's Arms Hotel in the main square.**
Above: **The Honeypot** – a deli and artisan food shop. It stocks 50 types of honey and 40 different cheeses, plus a wide range of local products.

HAWKSHEAD

Tucked away in a corner of the bustling main square, the Methodist chapel has been a place of worship since 1862. Originally a 16th-century cottage, it was gifted to the non-conformists in the area by a Mrs Satterthwaite and left to the Methodist Church after her husband's death. The unassuming building is claimed to be the oldest place used for Methodist worship in the world. Kept much as it was in the early 1900s, it is open every day for prayer and quiet meditation.

A narrow lane leading off the square nearby is called Flag Street because of the flagstones that cover a stream still flowing beneath them. Householders used to draw water from the stream when it was left open in the square.

Below: Minstrels Gallery Tearoom and the Methodist chapel. Flag Street goes off left.

▲ The Queen's Head, a tiny half-timbered inn at the southern end of Main Street, is claimed to be the oldest building in Hawkshead, dating to the late 16th century. The name refers to that of Queen Elizabeth I, who was on the throne when it was built.

Despite the crowds, I never tire of Hawkshead, with its cavalcade of attractive places to draw. I could spend a week sketching in the village and still find new scenes to capture.

169

HAWKSHEAD

▶ William Wordsworth arrived at Hawkshead school aged eight following his mother's death. He lodged in the care of Ann Tyson, firstly at a cottage in the village between 1779 and 1784, then at the hamlet of Colthouse on the outskirts of Hawkshead after the death of Mrs Tyson's husband. By all accounts William enjoyed his time at Hawkshead and wrote warmly of ice-skating, climbing and fishing. Sending an eight-year-old boy to school on the other side of the county and lodging him with an unrelated family would set all kinds of alarm bells ringing these days… Imagine the paperwork!

▶ The Church of St Michael stands on a grassy hill overlooking the village. The present building replaced an ancient chapel built in the 15th century. Rounded pillars and patterned arches inside echo Norman and Romanesque designs. The church is situated on a hill that provides superlative views across the village to the Lakeland fells beyond. The sandstone war memorial in the churchyard is based on the 11th-century cross in St Mary's churchyard, Gosforth.

▶ The Grammar School was founded in 1585 by Edwin Sandys, a local-born cleric who Queen Elizabeth made Archbishop of York. William Wordsworth attended the school between 1779 and 1787. The ground floor classroom retains many old desks featuring carvings done by old boys – including young Wordsworth. His initials are encased in glass and it has been suggested that his act of juvenile vandalism has saved the school for posterity by ensuring a steady stream of paying tourists. The school closed in 1909.

HAWKSHEAD

Above: Ann Tyson's Cottage, Colthouse.

▶ Hawkshead Hall was built just north of the village, from where the stewards of Furness Abbey took care of business. The original building was probably extensive, with various barns and cattle sheds. All that remains is an arched gateway and courthouse above. Rents were received here and wrongdoers tried. A gallows stood on a nearby hill.

CONISTON

Above: **Yewdale Road and the Yewdale fells.**
Below: **Houses over Church Beck bridge.**

Coniston

Well away from the A591 tourist track through Lakeland, Coniston attracts its fair share of visitors, but enjoys little of the attractiveness of Hawkshead. This is an old mining village plain and simple; the slate grey-green buildings and Victorian shop fronts are dominated by rugged fells and the settlement retains a rough-and-ready utilitarian appeal.

Mining in these fells stretches way back. Historians believe Coniston was probably the oldest mining area in the north of England, boasting some 2,000 years of intermittent working. Serious mining for copper and iron ore didn't start in earnest until the 16th century, reaching peak output around 1860. Slate quarries were opened on the Old Man of Coniston and at Tilberthwaite, attracting even more workers to the village – some from Bavaria. In 1859, the mines were linked to the coastal railway by a branch line to Broughton in Furness.

As is the way with boom times, they didn't last. By 1890 mining in the area had virtually ceased. Despite the loss of industrial business, the railway struggled on for another six decades, but after tourists abandoned it for the motor car, it finally closed in 1957.

CONISTON

Coniston shops are predictably of the gift, outdoor clothing and novelty variety, with a selection of inns and cafés to choose from. No-one comes to Coniston for the shopping, though coach parties remain well served.

Prominent in the village centre, the Black Bull, a 400-year-old former coaching inn, had the painter J. M. W. Turner as a guest in 1797. He made sketches of the crags above the village for paintings that now hang in The Tate, including the celebrated *Morning Amongst the Coniston Fells, Cumberland*.

The Ruskin Museum is an interesting place to spend a rainy day learning about John Ruskin's life, work and thoughts. Personal items of his are also on display – including a pair of socks. The museum charts Coniston's history through the ages, and includes a section on local crafts such as linen- and lace-making, which Ruskin promoted.

St Andrew's Church was built in 1819 on the site of a chapel that William Le Fleming of Coniston Hall had built in 1586. A chapel and vestry were added in 1891 when the church was completely restored. Sadly, it remains a dull, grey-stone building, gradually disappearing behind a screen of fir and yew trees.

John Ruskin and Donald Campbell are both buried in the churchyard, Ruskin beneath an ornate Anglo-Saxon-style cross, carved from local Tilberthwaite slate and designed by his friend William Collingwood.

Above: **Church Beck flows through – and occasionally floods – the village.**
Left: **The Black Bull and Yew Pike.**

CONISTON

Coniston Water

Though of substantial size – just over five miles long, almost half a mile wide and with a maximum depth of around 180ft – seen from the main A593 road Coniston Water is something of a disappointment. The lake is, instead, best seen from the narrow road along its eastern shore, with the Old Man of Coniston and neighbouring southern fells gathered together as a dramatic background.

For almost a century the lake was a busy industrial waterway, with iron ore shipped to be smelted in the many lakeside bloomeries fuelled by wood from hillside forests. Copper was transported south to the lake foot for transportation to Greenodd on the River Leven estuary. These days the lake is busy with all manner of leisure craft and tourist launches, but boat speeds limited to 10mph help keep the lake tranquil.

While exploring the Cumbria Way in 1996 I stayed overnight at Torver after my first day's walk from Ulverston. The next morning, I enjoyed a traditional B&B breakfast of

Below: **The Coniston fells from Brantwood.**

CONISTON

English fry-up with all the trimmings before joining the path along the western lakeside. With a full belly, the sun overhead, bird song in the trees and water lapping at my feet, it was a memorable three miles of wonder and contemplation. I re-entered the real world at Coniston Hall campsite. But even that was quiet. And the aroma of frying bacon of a morning never goes amiss in the great outdoors.

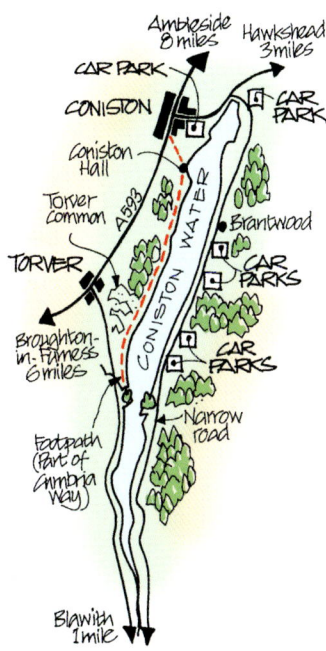

Donald Campbell 1921–67

Scarcely a Lakeland icon, but Campbell is forever associated with Coniston Water, where he died trying to break his own world water speed record of 276mph.

Millions watched TV coverage of Bluebird backflipping on the lake and heard Campbell's poignant last words: "I'm going! I'm gone!" His body was retrieved in 2001 and buried in St Andrew's churchyard.

Arthur Ransome 1884–1967

Born in Leeds, Ransome bought his first Lakes house in 1925. He started writing the first of his 12 *Swallows and Amazons* children's stories in 1929.

Five of them were exclusively set around Coniston Water and Windermere, and reflected his passions for sailing, camping and fishing.

CONISTON

John Ruskin 1819–1900

The leading English art critic of the Victorian era, Ruskin was also an art patron, draughtsman, watercolourist, philosopher, prominent social thinker and philanthropist. He was born to well-to-do Scottish parents in Bloomsbury, London. His father was a wine merchant with the sherry-importing company Domecq. John was especially close to his mother, who took lodgings to be near him when he went to study at Christ Church, Oxford.

Like many upper-middle-class families, the Ruskins travelled widely, and they visited Lakeland on numerous occasions. John wrote essays and poems about his experiences. He went on to write many books on art and became the first Slade Professor of Fine Art at Oxford.

In 1848 he married Euphemia Chalmers Gray, the daughter of family friends in Scotland. The marriage was a disaster and their divorce six years later became the talk of Victorian London.

His father died in 1852, with John inheriting the family estate. This enabled him to buy Brantwood and, at the age of 52, move permanently to the Lake District.

Managed by a charitable trust, Brantwood, on the east shore of Coniston Water, is open to the public as Ruskin requested. The rambling mansion retains much of his character, with nine rooms filled with fine paintings, beautiful furniture and personal treasures. Eight unique gardens spread up the wooded hillside, developed by Ruskin as he explored ideas for land management and horticulture.

The view across the lake to the Coniston fells is sensational. Ruskin had a turret built on the house from where he could sit and admire it.

Brantwood was originally built as a simple rough-cast cottage in about 1797, and had a history of radical, arty owners. The first, Gerald Massey, was a poet and philosopher. Then came W. V. Linton, who enlarged the cottage considerably and set up a printing press to publish *The English Republic*, a radical journal.

When Linton's marriage failed, Ruskin bought Brantwood from him for £1,500 without seeing it first. "Any place opposite Coniston Old Man must be beautiful," he said. Instead he found it "a mere shed of rotten timbers and loose stone". During the next 29 years, he invested thousands of pounds in it, adding to the building and stocking it with art treasures, including paintings by Turner, whom he championed. The estate was extended until it covered some 250 acres.

Despite increasing bouts of illness, Ruskin continued to write at Brantwood, producing numerous booklets and pamphlets on a variety of subjects.

Above: Brantwood from the lake shore.

CONISTON

Built in 1856, the steam yacht Gondola sailed on Coniston until it was decommissioned in 1936. After running aground during a storm in the 1960s she was left to rot in the lake. Eventually, the National Trust rebuilt the vessel and brought her back into service in 1980.

Originally coal-burning, Gondola has embraced sustainability and is now fuelled by compressed-sawdust logs. She carries up to 86 passengers in considerable luxury with a stop-off at Brantwood.

Two even more eco-friendly launches – Ruskin and Ransome – are solar-powered wooden vessels providing regular services around the lake. They sail specialist routes, one associated with Donald Campbell, the other around southern parts of the lake used as settings for Ransome's *Swallows and Amazons* books. Both routes also call at Brantwood.

Above: The steam yacht Gondola.

▲ Bank Ground Farm snuggles up to the southern lakeside and was Arthur Ransome's inspiration for Holly Howe, playground of the Walker children. The farm featured in the 1974 film version of *Swallows and Amazons*. Its gem of a tearoom has fabulous views and food to match.

▶ Coniston Old Hall stands in isolation on the lakeside, its round chimneys – each as wide at the base as a normal room – a landmark for miles around. Built by the Le Fleming family, one of the area's largest landowners, the 15th-century cruck-framed building once contained a great banqueting hall, fine oak panelling and huge stone fireplaces. When the family abandoned Coniston for Rydal the Hall fell into ruin. In 1915 it was patched up as a rudimentary farmhouse. The banqueting hall became a barn and a causeway was built to provide access for haywagons. The building is now owned by the National Trust, which has done some renovation, but – for now – the Hall remains closed to the public.

Ravenglass & Eskdale

Fells, Romans and countryside

ESKDALE

The valley of Eskdale is 12 glorious miles long, with scenic delights ranging from the plains and sand dunes of Ravenglass to the dramatic mountain pass of Esk Hause at the head of the valley. Set at the southwestern extremity of the National Park, Eskdale is the only part of it that makes contact with the sea. Thanks in part to the Sellafield nuclear plant seven miles north of Ravenglass, it also enjoys the only mainline rail station within Park boundaries.

The main road into Eskdale crosses scarcely four miles of the valley itself, with the westerly stretch to Eskdale Green actually in neighbouring Miterdale. Approaching the great mountain barrier at the dale head, the road veers east to Hardknott Pass, leaving Upper Eskdale as the exclusive preserve of sheep, shepherds and adventurous walkers.

The River Esk rises among a dramatic bowl of fells that surround Great Moss, twisting and winding down the valley – a silver thread through miniature gorges, flood plain meadows and oak woodland.

Here the fells lie back, forming a pleasing background. As if reluctant to leave the valley, the Esk performs a series of tortuous twists before abruptly turning north under the railway at Eskmeals Viaduct to reach the open sea at Ravenglass.

Above. Upper Eskdale from the slopes of Harter Fell.
Top: Ravenglass village green.

Ravenglass

The isolated settlement of Ravenglass is sometimes marketed as 'Cumbria's oldest sea port', but it's many centuries since it did any serious sea trading. More romantically, it was a smuggler's haven in the 18th century – despite the best efforts of a resident coastwatcher and an excise man.

The main street is virtually the village's *only* street, ending with a ramp onto the beach. A heavy door can be closed across the end of the street to keep out high tides.

The beach is not bucket-and-spade sand; instead it is formed of the silted estuary of three rivers: the Irt, Mite and Esk. The backs of the houses on the seaward side and a defensive sea wall rise from the beach in a gloriously haphazard manner, as though growing out of the beach. Ladders and rudimentary stone steps descend through rickety doorways from back yards where washing flaps in the wind. A rusting anchor is embedded in the shingle and gulls cry overhead. I love it.

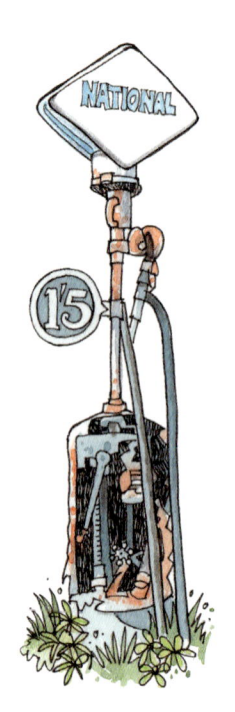

Above: **The Pharoahs' petrol pump.**
Below: **Ravenglass houses overlooking the beach.**

Many of the houses in Ravenglass have been sensitively restored and gentrified on the street side, with colourful gardens and pot plants amongst the cobblestones.

One building used to house J. A. Pharoah & Son's shop and garage. The family also made clogs and repaired shoes. An ancient petrol pump has been left to rust outside the garage site in the The Pharoahs' memory. The price tag on the pump reads 'one shilling and five pence' (presumably per gallon), which would be seven and a half pence in today's currency. Gasp!

Part-time residents are not just a modern phenomenon. In 1976, 15 of the 69 habitable dwellings in Main Street were reported to be occupied only for short periods.

I've been to Ravenglass a number of times, but I've yet to be there when the tide's in. I have to rely, instead, on my OS map to confirm that the Irish Sea is indeed out there beyond the wasteland of ever-shifting beaches, rivers and sand dunes.

RAVENGLASS

The Romans established a port at what is now Ravenglass in around AD49. They called it Glennaventa, and it was the western terminus of the road over Hardknott and Wrynose Passes from the outpost at Ambleside. It became the most important harbour on the northwest coast, with the number of Roman roads radiating from it indicating the considerable onward movement of goods and troops.

A fort was built south of the present village and some of its bathhouse survives. Known as Walls Castle, the stone construction is one of Britain's largest and best-preserved Roman remains. Parts of the wall are 12ft high, with pink mortar rending still visible.

When the Roman Empire crumbled at the end of the fourth century the invaders withdrew and Ravenglass was left in peace – until the next sea invasion around 900AD, this time by Vikings.

Home to the Pennington family since at least 1208, Muncaster Castle stands on the

> **Ruskin called the view from Muncaster Castle the 'gateway to paradise'.**

wooded lower slopes of Muncaster Fell, east of Ravenglass. The present edifice of towers, battlements and mullioned windows was built by Anthony Salvin during the 1860s for the fourth Lord Muncaster. It's open to the public with a noted display of rhododendrons and azaleas in its 77-acre garden. There's also a hawk and owl centre.

In my opinion, the view up Eskdale from the Castle terrace beats those azaleas. From this elevated position, the eye soars over woodlands to the Esk and the cluster of mountains beyond. Ruskin called this panorama the 'gateway to paradise'.

The castle is reputed to be haunted by several ghosts, including 'Tom Fool', who is known for directing travellers into the quicksands of the estuary. But my favourite is the headless carpenter. I drew many headless ghosts during my time as a kids' comics artist, but have yet to see if the Muncaster apparition carries a head under his arm in classic comic strip fashion. I hope he does.

181

LA'AL RATTY

La'al Ratty

Towards the end of the 19th century, rich deposits of haematite were discovered in Eskdale. Boot was established as a mining village and in 1875 a three-foot-gauge railway was laid to carry iron ore down-valley to Ravenglass, seven miles away. The mining company went bust two years later, but the railway struggled on until 1913 when it was dismantled.

Two years later a tiny 15-inch-gauge line was relaid on the same trackbed, with steam trains carrying goods, passengers and mail into the valley. After the First World War, granite quarries reopened in Eskdale and for a while the line became industrial again.

Those quarries closed in 1953 and a second period of decline set in.

That was arrested in 1960, when a preservation society bought the railway at auction and turned it into the popular visitor attraction of today, with five working steam locomotives and seven request stops along the valley. The Ravenglass & Eskdale Railway is one of the oldest and longest narrow-gauge railways in England. Its affectionate nickname, La'al Ratty, is thought to refer to the line's pioneer engineer called Ratcliffe.

Above: **A La'al Ratty steam loco.**

Left: **La'al Ratty at Muncaster Mill, once a water-powered corn mill and now a private residence.**

Eskdale Green

The small and peaceful village of Eskdale Green is set on the lower slopes of Muncaster Fell, some five miles up-valley from Ravenglass. Several of the houses are built of Eskdale granite, the most handsome of Lakeland rock, with a fabulously flecked sparkle of pink and blue. There's also an excellent shop. But apart from a La'al Ratty train station at each end of the village there are no other facilities.

An imposing mansion, Gatehouse, was built in the village during 1896 as a country retreat for Lord Rea, a Liverpool coal and shipping tycoon. Since 1950 it has been owned by The Outward Bound Trust, which provides a range of outdoor pursuits. The grounds and lake were designed by the famous landscape architect Thomas Mawson of Windermere. I once peeped into the grounds, where two gangs of noisy youngsters were trying to push an immense football over each other.

Above: Part of Gatehouse.
Below: King George IV inn.

▲ King George IV inn stands alone on the outskirts of the village, not far from the Outward Bound school – handy for inmates to nip over the wall for a drink. It dates back to the 16th century, with an even older cellar and the remains of a Roman bathhouse. Way back it was called 'Tatty Garth', referencing a nearby potato field. Then for a while it was 'The King of Prussia', which was swiftly changed when war broke out in 1914.

I stayed overnight at the King George IV inn when researching my *Lakeland Villages* book in 1986, driving over the high moorland country from Ulpha in the Duddon valley. On the way, I passed Devoke Water, which is as large as Rydal Water, but is still classed as a tarn. There are reckoned to be around 400 Bronze Age settlements around the area, though I never counted them all.

I did stop, however, when I saw a sheep upside down in a ditch by the road, frantically waving its legs. I'm no James Herriot, but I quickly diagnosed that in this remote place the sheep was in trouble and needed help.

What I hadn't considered was this was a big and heavy animal... and it didn't want to be helped. A struggle ensued, and eventually the sheep struggled to its feet and wandered off without a backward look – or even a baa of thanks.

When I got back to my car I realised my hands were covered in a greasy substance. I discovered later that it was lanolin, produced as waterproofing by the sebaceous glands of the sheep's skin. Lanolin is also used in human skin-care and the cosmetics industry. It explained why my hands were so smooth for the rest of the day.

Boot

How does anywhere set in one of the loveliest Lakeland valleys acquire such an ugly name? The question turns out to be more interesting than the answer. The name derives from the Middle English term for a bend. And Eskdale does bend here, so that's reasonable.

The settlement developed out of the 19th-century mining industry, becoming a hub of activity in the valley: packhorse trails crossed here; a corpse road over Eskdale Moor to Wasdale Head passed through; and the railway from the coast at Ravenglass ended.

As productivity at the mines and quarries declined, Boot changed from a mining to a tourist village. The railway was shortened and is now a major tourist attraction, terminating at Dalegarth, a couple of fields away.

A packhorse bridge over Whillan Beck leads to an old mill, dating back to 1578 – now the last remaining working water-powered corn mill in the Lake District National Park. In 1970 Cumbria County Council restored the mill to working order, and a group of local enthusiasts took it over in 2006 to run as a visitor attraction. Boot has two inns, a selection of holiday lets and the inevitable sprinkling of second homes.

Above: The bridge over Whillan Beck and the corn mill at Boot.
Below: Boot looking east to Harter Fell.

Harter Fell overlooks the village from the east, compelling attention. Rising alone from the tree-lined River Esk to 2,142ft, this is a true mountain, clad in bracken lower down, a belt of heather higher up, then crowned with clean-cut ramparts of rock. Alfred Wainwright admired the mountain, noting: "Not many fells can be described as beautiful, but the word fits Harter Fell."

St Catherine's, the 17th-century parish church of Eskdale, occupies a solitary site on the bank of the River Esk. In the churchyard there's an impressive headstone for Tommy Dobson, master and founder of the Eskdale and Ennerdale Foxhounds, carved with his genial effigy.

Beyond the simple local granite church the river is a delight, with deep pools to bathe in and narrow canyons through which centuries of rushing water have polished the rock to glistening smoothness.

A walk up the river leads to Stanley Ghyll Force, a 60ft-high waterfall in a dramatic deep and narrow gorge. The romantic Victorians declared it the finest waterfall in Lakeland and even paid to see the spectacle in spate. Today, the waterfall is free to enjoy for anyone prepared for a short walk.

UPPER ESKDALE

As its name suggests, The Woolpack inn – furthest up the dale of Eskdale hostelries – once catered for the packhorse trade using Hardknott Pass. It performs a similar task today, enabling motorists to gird their loins before climbing the pass, or steady their nerves having just descended. The inn's also popular with walkers, and many popular routes start/end here.

A cattle-grid in the road marks the end of meadowed Eskdale and the start of Hardknott Pass over the open fell.

Hardknott Fort stands on the lower slopes of the pass, built by the Romans during the first century AD to protect their road from Ambleside to Ravenglass. Its grassy shelf makes a superb defensive position, with high mountains to the east and a view straight down the Esk valley to the sea. Not all of the remains are Roman work; some are controversial reconstructions to indicate scale. However, the views of some of Lakeland's greatest mountains – including the Scafells and Bowfell – *are* genuine, and stunning.

Above: **The Woolpack.**
Below: **The head of Eskdale from Boot.**

Brotherilkeld is Eskdale's remotest and likely oldest farmstead, a Norse outpost in the tenth century and a Furness Abbey grange in the 12th. The present 17th-century farm has been occupied by the same family for more than a century, rearing Herdwick sheep on the upper Eskdale fellsides.

A one-and-a half-hour-long film of their sheep being gathered in for clipping was shown on BBC TV in 2020 to critical acclaim.

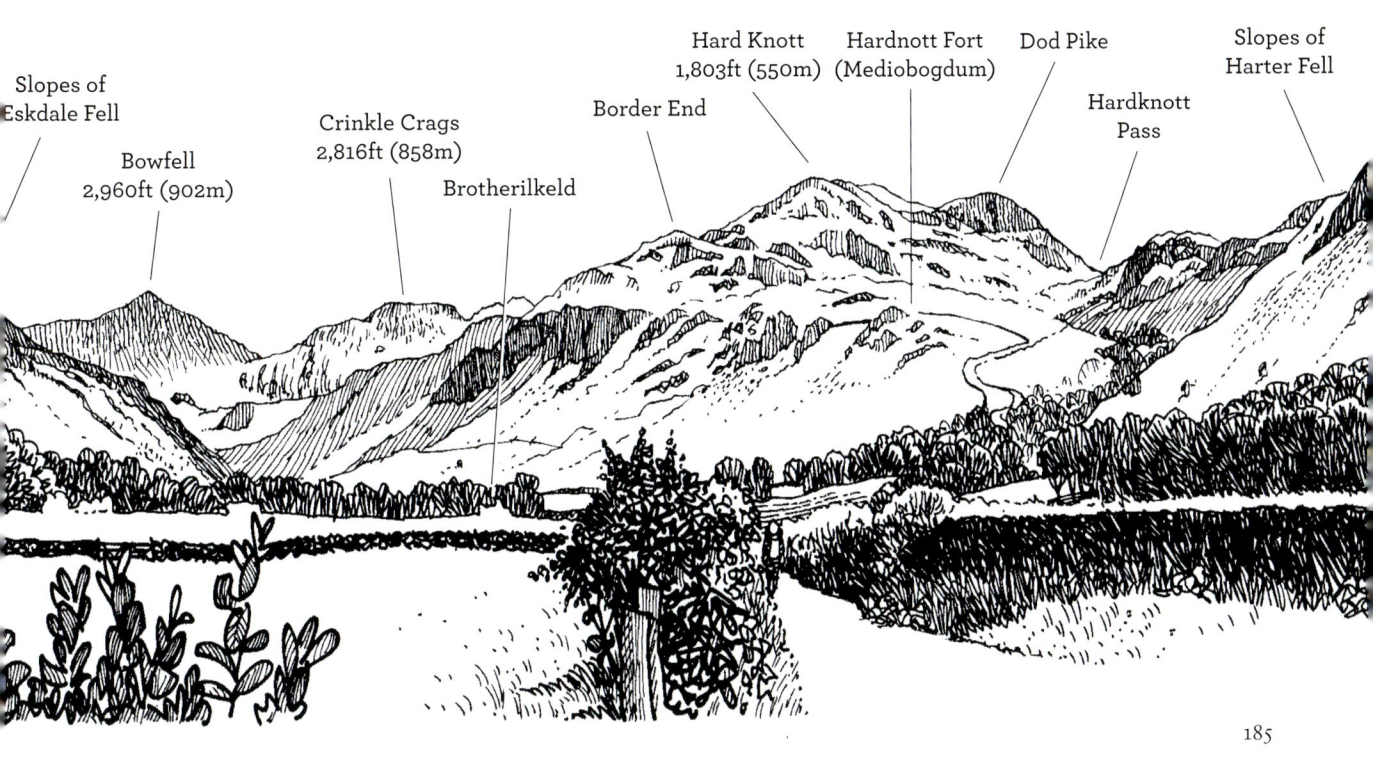

Slopes of Eskdale Fell

Bowfell 2,960ft (902m)

Crinkle Crags 2,816ft (858m)

Brotherilkeld

Border End

Hard Knott 1,803ft (550m)

Hardnott Fort (Mediobogdum)

Dod Pike

Hardknott Pass

Slopes of Harter Fell

Wasdale

Highest, deepest, biggest, smallest – and my saddest visit

Wasdale is tucked away in the remote southwest corner of Lakeland with sensational scenery and a clutch of superlatives to match. The most dramatic and haunting of the lakes, Wast Water lies near the head of the dale. The lake is around three miles long, half a mile wide, and deep – very deep; the deepest in England.

Overshadowing the lake, in every sense, are the Wast Water Screes, an almost 2,000ft-high wall of shattered rock, running nearly the entire length of the southwest shore,

Below: Wast Water and the Wasdale fells.

- Bowderdale
- Yewbarrow 2,060ft (628m)
- Wasdale Head
- Mosedale
- Great Gable 2,949ft (899m)
- Sty Head
- Lingmell Gill
- Lingmell 2,649ft (807m)

tumbling in a series of fan-shaped down-slopes to the lake bed 259ft below the surface. The magnificent desolation is extraordinary, and oddly sinister.

The mountain composition at the head of the valley – Yewbarrow, Great Gable and Lingmell – was for a while adopted as the emblem of the Lake District National Park. Scafell Pike, England's highest mountain, is rightly dominant, with Scafell a knobbly counterpoint.

Up to four million gallons of water a day are piped from Wast Water to the Sellafield nuclear facility as an 'industrial water supply'.

Scafell Pike
3,210ft (978m)

Scafell
3,162ft (964m)

Scafell Crag

The Screes

Illgill Head
1,983ft (604m)

WASDALE

Above: **Nether Wasdale.**

Wasdale ends at Wasdale Head. Where the valley *begins* is unclear. I'm sure there must be an official border, but for me it's at Nether Wasdale, an unassuming hamlet with a couple of inns and a view of the Wast Water Screes that most of us would relish in our back garden.

The mile or so from here to the lake is through pastoral Lakeland, where bracken wraps rocky outcrops, sheep fleck open fields, woodland crowns low hills and ancient stone walls line the winding rollercoaster road. There's no hint of the drama lying ahead.

We visited Wast Water in September 2020, when a big surprise awaited – but this time it wasn't the screes that stunned us. Instead, emerging from the woodland around Wasdale Hall we entered Motorhome City.

The open moorland that runs down to the lakeside was packed with motorhomes for as far as my widened eyes could see. Figures in wet suits ran to and from the lake. Paddle boards, kayaks and swimmers spread out across the water. Barbecues were fired up and teenagers played football.

The brooding atmosphere of the lake that I'd enjoyed for years was shattered – by people enjoying themselves!

The COVID-19 pandemic regulations had been loosened at the time, and we were being let out after months of staying at home, 'locked down'. Wast Water is the only lake where you can park unrestricted at the lakeside, so who could blame the motorhome crowd for flocking there? Well… me I suppose. We didn't stay long.

WASDALE HEAD

Wasdale Head

With only an inn, a farm, a church and a scattering of cottages, the fame of this remote hamlet lies in the surrounding mountains, where the sport of rock climbing was born in the late 19th century. The inn became its unofficial headquarters, attracting professional types from the industrial towns and cities – as well as plenty of Oxbridge students – looking for adventure. Wearing plimsolls and tweed suits, they scrambled up rock towers with bits of old towrope for protection, establishing many of the classic routes that today are classified as 'very severe'.

The inn's first landlord was Will Ritson, one of a long line of Wasdale statesmen and a larger-than-life character. His ability to tell tall tales while keeping a straight face earned him the title of 'World's Biggest Liar'. A competition to find his successor was held for many years at Wasdale Head. The Bridge Inn at Santon Bridge now hosts the event.

The surrounding mountains are remarkable – great lumps of volcanic rock, sculpted by glacial action. Jagged bands of crags circle Great Gable, the dale-head superstar. Surrounding fells have their own characters: Yewbarrow reminds me of an upturned ship; Scafell Pike has a regal air; and its slightly smaller sibling, Scafell, is all craggy energy – begging for attention.

Above: Wasdale Head Hotel.
Below left: Bridge Inn, Santon Bridge.
Below right: Great Gable and the packhorse bridge over Mosedale Beck.

WASDALE HEAD

▶ St Olaf's Church is sometimes claimed to be the smallest parish church in England – though other claimants are available. The building is certainly diminutive and is likely over 400 years old. Walls of rendered Wasdale stone and an enclosure of 32 yew trees give the place a sombre mood. Climbers killed on the surrounding fells lie in the tiny churchyard.

For many years the dead from Wasdale had to be transported five miles to St Catherine's Church in Eskdale for burial via the corpse road over bleak Burnmoor. St Olaf's did not have a graveyard until 1901.

Stones washed down from the fells in ancient times are all over Upper Wasdale. Some have been collected into great heaps in the fields. Those that haven't been worn smooth have been built into substantial walls.

Dry-stone walls are a feature throughout Lakeland, but nowhere are they more in evidence than at Wasdale Head. They seem to be everywhere, dividing the modest area of valley-head farmland into a green patchwork quilt, best appreciated from above.

Most Lakeland walls were built by bands of itinerant wallers and date from the Enclosure Act of 1801, when more intensive farming methods were introduced – even in remote backwaters like Wasdale.

The settlement's remoteness was eased in 1977 when electricity was brought up the valley after a furious row over the possible introduction of electricity pylons into the landscape. Good sense eventually prevailed, and the cables were laid underground, with the momentous switch-on covered by national television.

Left: **Wasdale Head from the slopes of Wasdale Fell.**

WASDALE HEAD

◀ The interior of St Olaf's is a delight. Some of the wooden roof beams are said to have come from Viking ships wrecked on the Solway coast. There are three small windows, a stone floor and sturdy oak pews. It's disrespectful I know, but all the unpolished woodwork reminds me of an old cow shed. St Olaf is the patron saint of Norway – an indication of the church's Norse heritage.

Below: Bull Crag towers over the hamlet of Greendale, across the lake from The Screes.

▲ A delicate etching of Napes Needle in the south window of St Olaf's is dedicated to members of the Fell & Rock Climbing Club. The inscription (based on Psalm 121) reads: "I will lift up mine eyes unto the hills from whence cometh my strength."

The passes

Tracks and pathways have criss-crossed the Lake District since Neolithic times. When the Romans invaded in AD43, they developed a road network to move troops and goods around. Many of their original routes survive to this day.

Packhorses were used extensively during the 18th century, when Lakeland industries – particularly mining and quarrying – were at their most productive. Higher quality turnpike roads were steadily built from the late 1700s, when horse-drawn wagons and stagecoaches made an appearance.

Towards the end of the 19th century wealthy tourists began venturing into the area in significant numbers and required decent roads for their carriages. The advent of the motorised vehicle escalated visitor numbers further – first charabancs of the early 1900s and latterly the private car.

Roads over Lakeland passes are now largely visitor-friendly – though some remain a challenge, with hairy moments at busy times and in winter conditions.

Below: **The Ullswater side of Kirkstone Pass.**

Kirkstone Pass

Situated on the main A592 road between Ullswater and Windermere, Kirkstone Pass is the highest motor pass in the Lake District, climbing to 1,489ft (454m) and with spectacular scenes along the way.

From Brothers Water, the road begins to twist and climb past a sensational view of the Dovedale crags. This side is steep – 25% in places – but the road is broad and sweeping. The long descent to Windermere begins in an airy mountain setting between Red Screes and Caudale Moor, and ends in the pastoral paradise of Troutbeck, with terrific views along the way.

Kirkstone Pass Inn stands at the summit of the pass. Once an important coaching stop, it now mainly caters for tourists enjoying the highest location of any public house in Cumbria, and the third highest in England.

KIRKSTONE PASS

Dating back to 1496, the building had the tall part added in the early 1800s as a coach house high enough to accommodate the carriages of the day. Around the 1950s the extension became a garage with petrol pumps. Now it's been converted into a cottage. There's also a budget bothy attached that sleeps 12 (bring your own sleeping bag) with central heating and a hot shower... A bothy for wimps, basically.

Creditably green, the inn collects water from the fell behind the building, while a wind turbine generates most of its electricity.

To get to Kirkstone Pass from Ambleside you drive up a very narrow and surprisingly steep road through the Peggy Hill residential area of town. Just when you think the climb is never going to end, the road levels out and you're in wild fell country.

Above: **Kirkstone Pass Inn.**
Below: **The Ambleside side of Kirkstone Pass with Red Screes and 'The Struggle' up to the inn.**

The steepest part of the road is a final stretch up the so-called 'Struggle' to the inn. This used to be a popular ride out for Victorian visitors to Ambleside. I sometimes wonder if the carriage driver ever warned his paying customers before they set off that they'd have to get out and walk alongside the horses up the last part.

HONISTER PASS

Honister Pass

With gradients of one-in-four and an altitude of 1,167ft (356m), Honister Pass, between Borrowdale and Buttermere, is one of the steepest and highest in the district.

From Borrowdale there's a short, steep climb alongside excitable Hause Gill to a wide summit plateau.

Below: The Buttermere side of the pass.
Below right: Honister Slate Mine entrance.

The descent plunges down a fabulous rock-strewn gill below the craggy heights of Fleetwith Pike into Buttermere.

The entrance to Honister Slate Mine marks the start of the Buttermere descent. The huddle of unlovely buildings add nothing to the scene, but they do retain the site's long-standing industrial heritage; the light-green slate mined at Honister is thought to be around 450 million years old.

By 1890 production at Honister mine had reached 3,000 tons a year, and more than 100 men were employed in often appalling conditions underground. In those days the mine was so isolated that miners lived on-site during the week and messages to the company offices in Keswick were sent by carrier pigeon.

Business gradually declined and by the 1980s a complete shutdown was threatened. However, in 1997 the mine was reopened by new owners Bill Taylor and Mark Weir as an adventure tourist attraction, with Honister Slate (or, more correctly, Westmorland Green Slate) also back in commercial production.

Visitors can now enjoy an exhilarating Via Ferrata following the original miners' route across the exposed face of Fleetwith Pike using a fixed cableway, ladders and supports. If that's not scary enough, there's an 'Infinity Bridge' – the longest wire bridge in the country – which crosses a 2,000ft chasm.

Mark Weir died in 2011 when his helicopter crashed near the mine.

Whinlatter Pass

As Lakeland passes go, Whinlatter is not particularly high, just exceeding 1,000ft (305m) as it traverses the five miles or so between Lorton and Braithwaite.

Most of the pass road travels through Whinlatter Forest Park, a mountain forest planted in response to timber shortages following the First World War. Whinlatter now encompasses more than 3,000 acres of pine, larch and spruce.

The park is home to all manner of outdoor activities, with nine walking trails, three cycle routes, play areas and waymarked running tracks. The Forest Centre has seasonal exhibitions on the forest's wildlife, and during the nesting season (Easter to August) you can watch the wild ospreys at Bassenthwaite on a live video nest-cam link.

For much of the route over Whinlatter the outlook is restricted by trees, but a mile out of Braithwaite there's a clearing with a panoramic view of Skiddaw and Bassenthwaite. Derwent Water is just out of sight on the right. In particularly wet periods it is not uncommon for the flat lands between the two lakes to flood, and after Storm Desmond the extreme rainfall merged them into a single stretch of water.

Above: Entering the forest at Scawgill Bridge.
Below: Skiddaw and Bassenthwaite Lake from Whinlatter.

DUNMAIL RAISE

Dunmail Raise

Given that it rises no higher than 781ft (238m) and is only about two miles long, calling the Raise a 'pass' elevates it to an unmerited level. However, it does represent a significant cultural and topographical divide between north and south Lakeland. Some say (northerners) that the south is soft and chocolate box, while others (southerners) consider the north to be wild and untamed. Regarding the landscape, there's a lot of truth in both views. The ethnic aspect is a matter of opinion – though I know where my roots are.

The Raise, an ancient route since the Stone Age, is named after Dunmail, the last Norse King of Cumbria, who was defeated in battle on this hillside in AD945 by the combined forces of the Saxon King Edmund I and Malcolm, King of the Scots.

Legend has it that Dunmail was killed in the battle and Cumbrian prisoners were forced to collect rocks and pile them on top of his body, forming a cairn. Survivors fled with the Crown of Cumberland, climbing to Grisedale Tarn below Helvellyn, where they threw it into the depths to be kept safe until the king would rise again to lead them.

Sadly, the story was scuppered when a spoilsport history geek observed that Dunmail actually lived for another 30 years after the battle! Nevertheless, a pile of stones still graces the summit of the Raise.

Below: The 'Lion and the lamb' rock formation.

▲ The Grasmere side of the Raise climbs steadily from the Traveller's Rest, originally a 16th-century coaching inn. The road – the main A591 highway through the Lakes – is of broad three-car width, with a short stretch of dual carriageway across the top. During the climb, it's traditional to glance at the summit of Helm Crag on the left-hand skyline, where rocks form a silhouette of the famous 'Lion and the Lamb' – as pointed out to passengers by generations of coach drivers. The road narrows on the northern side, slowing boy racers, and meanders down to the woods around Thirlmere. Parts of the road south of the reservoir were washed away during Storm Desmond in 2015. It was closed for six months, severing this key historic artery through the Lakes.

Newlands Hause

Rising to around 1,093ft (333m), Newlands Hause between Braithwaite and Buttermere is high point of the most prominent minor road that emerges from the enchanting Newlands valley. It's not the most challenging drive of the Lakeland passes, but as the narrow road snakes out of Braithwaite and crosses the eastern flanks of Barrow, Causey Pike and Knott Rigg, it offers an ever-changing viewpoint over Cat Bells, Maiden Moor and Robinson across the valley.

At first, the road out of Braithwaite follows Newlands Beck through pastoral country, but after crossing a cattle-grid the landscape becomes ever-steeper and more wild.

The Buttermere side of the pass is just as narrow, but steeper, sweeping down across the north flanks of High Snockrigg. The great bulk of Whiteless Pike dominates across the gully of Sail Beck. There's a small car park on the Hause summit with Moss Force waterfall – impressive in spate – just a short walk across the fellside.

Top: The cattlegrid start.
Above left: The Swinside Inn, an excellent hostelry.
Above right: Braithwaite village shop on the road to Newlands.

Left: Approaching the Hause summit, Moss Force to the left.
Below: The Buttermere descent.

Wrynose Pass

Notoriously steep and narrow, Wrynose twists and climbs to a 1,281ft-high (390m) plateau summit, where there's parking and the Three Shires Stone that used to mark the meeting point of the boundaries of Lancashire, Cumberland and Westmorland.

On parts of the ascent from Little Langdale it's impossible for two vehicles to pass – although passing places are provided. Rule of the road gives right of way to those ascending, though not everyone agrees, and reversing up or down steep slopes with restricted vision is par for the course. The descent to Cockley Beck is more twisty but less steep. There's also a grand view to the head of the Duddon and to Hardknott Pass – if nerves allow you a quick glance.

Right: **The descent to Cockley Beck.**
Left: **The Three Shires Stone.**

◀ Cockley Beck is a small hamlet established during the 16th century around the mining of copper ore. The farmhouse was built in the 1860s and is now a National Trust property. A self-catering holiday cottage is attached. The delightful Duddon valley drops south from Cockley Beck to the Duddon Sands at Foxfield. Without a lake, and difficult to access, the upper Duddon is well off the tourist trail, but much loved by Lakeland purists. Wordsworth was a fan, writing 34 sonnets about the valley and its river.

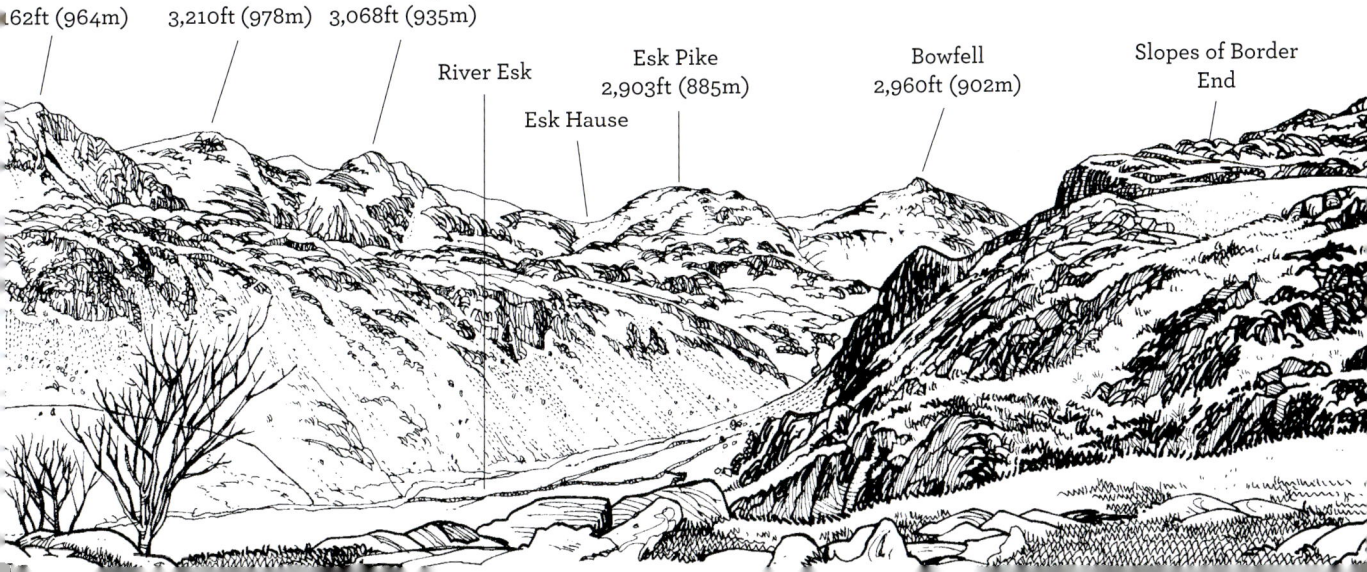

HARDKNOTT PASS

Hardknott Pass

Climbing to 1,291ft (394m), with 30%-steep gradients, sharp bends and a hair-raising sheer drop on one side soon after leaving Cockley Beck, Hardknott is often described as Lakeland's 'most exciting' road. It depends on your temperament, I suppose. However, with Wrynose included, the two passes present a considerable challenge for your average motorist. A steady nerve, good brakes and a willingness to back down – in all senses – are essential. You also have to keep a wary look out for cyclists, joggers, walkers and stray sheep as you progress.

Things become more relaxed at the small car park near the Roman Fort on the western slopes of Hard Knott fell, where it's worth stopping for a stroll over the fellside for a look at the Roman remains and a view of the Scafells – which are far more impressive.

Wrynose and Hardknott Passes were solidified in the first century AD by the Romans as part of a supply route between Ambleside and their port at Ravenglass. The Hardknott fort is superbly positioned to defend the route with a view down Eskdale to the coast and high crags to the east.

Right: **Hardknott from the Roman fort.**
Below: **The Scafells.**

Scafell 62ft (964m)
Scafell Pike 3,210ft (978m)
Ill Crag 3,068ft (935m)
River Esk
Esk Hause
Esk Pike 2,903ft (885m)
Bowfell 2,960ft (902m)
Slopes of Border End

About the author

Jim Watson was born in Penrith and brought up in Pooley Bridge and Threlkeld during the 1940s and 50s. He left the area to train as an engineering draughtsman in Rugby before becoming a freelance illustrator, cartoonist and writer.

He has drawn cartoons for various comics and produced a variety of work for publishers, magazines, greetings card companies and advertising agencies.

Jim has written and illustrated 19 books, eight of them on the Lake District and one a guide to the Cumbria Way. Others include collections of climbing and walking cartoons, a guide to architectural walks around London, and two self-published books of country walks in the Rugby area. *Lakeland Walker and Cumbria Magazine* publish his cartoon strips.

Despite having lived away from Lakeland for 60 years, Jim still considers himself a Cumberland lad.

PENRITH'S
THREE-SCREEN
CINEMAS
ALHAMBRA
LONSDALE
CINEMAS
CINEMA

My Lakeland: A local lad's illustrated life

Written and illustrated by Jim Watson © 2022.
Edited by David Felton.
Proofread by Fin O'Súilleabháin.
Designed by Andrew Chapman.

Printed by Latitude.

Published March 2022 by Jake Island Ltd,
3 Brunt How, Loughrigg, Cumbria, LA22 9HE.

All rights reserved.

ISBN 978-1-9998940-9-2

No part of this publication may be reproduced, stored in retrieval systems or transmitted in any form or by any means, electronic, mechanical, photocopying, recording or otherwise without the prior written permission of the publisher and copyright holder.

My Lakeland: A local lad's illustrated life is an Inspired by Lakeland title.

For news and other publications, including *The Lake District Quiz Book* and *The Lake District in 101 Maps & Infographics* see inspiredbylakeland.co.uk

INSPIRED BY LAKELAND

MIX
Paper from responsible sources
FSC® C014138